Current **CONTROVERSIES**

The Rights of Animals

DATE DUE

JUL 0 7 2009	
OCT 0 8 2009	
NOV 1 2 2009	
JUN 0 1 2010	
JUL 2 7 2010	
FEB 2 1 2013	
SEP 2 2 2016	

Other Books in the Current Controversies Series

CURRENT CONTROVERSIES

| The Rights of Animals

Debra A. Miller, Book Editor

GREENHAVEN PRESS
A part of Gale, Cengage Learning

GALE
CENGAGE Learning

Detroit • New York • San Francisco • New Haven, Conn • Waterville, Maine • London

GALE
CENGAGE Learning

Christine Nasso, *Publisher*
Elizabeth Des Chenes, *Managing Editor*

© 2009 Greenhaven Press, a part of Gale, Cengage Learning

Gale and Greenhaven Press are registered trademarks used herein under license.

For more information, contact:
Greenhaven Press
27500 Drake Rd.
Farmington Hills, MI 48331-3535
Or you can visit our Internet site at gale.cengage.com

Articles in Greenhaven Press anthologies are often edited for length to meet page requirements. In addition, original titles of these works are changed to clearly present the main thesis and to explicitly indicate the author's opinion. Every effort is made to ensure that Greenhaven Press accurately reflects the original intent of the authors. Every effort has been made to trace the owners of copyrighted material.

Cover image © Christian Anderl, 2008. Used under license from Shutterstock.com.

LIBRARY OF CONGRESS CATALOGING-IN-PUBLICATION DATA

The rights of animals / Debra A. Miller, book editor.
   p. cm. -- (Current controversies)
   Includes bibliographical references and index.
   ISBN 978-0-7377-4146-9 (hardcover)
   ISBN 978-0-7377-4147-6 (pbk.)
   1. 1. Animal rights--Juvenile literature. I. I. Miller, Debra A.
   HV4708.R543 2008
   179'.3--dc22
                                                         2008021554

Printed in the United States of America
1 2 3 4 5 6 7 12 11 10 09 08

Contents

Chapter 1: Should Animals Have Rights?

Joseph Lubinski

Animal rights and animal welfare advocates seek to advance the protections animals have under the law, while those opposed to animal rights believe that existing laws already provide adequate protections for animals and that rights should be reserved for human beings.

Yes: Animals Should Have Rights

Tom Regan

It is fundamentally wrong to view animals as human resources to be eaten, manipulated, or exploited for sport or money because animals, like humans, have inherent value. Nothing but the total abolition of animal agriculture, research, and hunting will guarantee animal rights.

Lesli Bisgould

All animals, including humans, are complex creatures, each with a special type of intelligence. Differences between animals and humans are not morally relevant to deciding who is entitled to basic, fundamental rights, such as the right to live and the right not be used for another's interests.

Chapter 2: Does the Food Industry Mistreat Animals?

Chapter 3: Is Animal Medical Experimentation Justified?

Yes: Animal Medical Experimentation Is Justified

No: Animal Medical Experimentation Is Not Justified

Chapter 4: Should It Be Allowed for Animals to Be Used for Entertainment?

Foreword

By definition, controversies are "discussions of questions in which opposing opinions clash" (Webster's Twentieth Century Dictionary Unabridged). Few would deny that controversies are a pervasive part of the human condition and exist on virtually every level of human enterprise. Controversies transpire between individuals and among groups, within nations and between nations. Controversies supply the grist necessary for progress by providing challenges and challengers to the status quo. They also create atmospheres where strife and warfare can flourish. A world without controversies would be a peaceful world; but it also would be, by and large, static and prosaic.

The Series' Purpose

The purpose of the *Current Controversies* series is to explore many of the social, political, and economic controversies dominating the national and international scenes today. Titles selected for inclusion in the series are highly focused and specific. For example, from the larger category of criminal justice, *Current Controversies* deals with specific topics such as police brutality, gun control, white collar crime, and others. The debates in *Current Controversies* also are presented in a useful, timeless fashion. Articles and book excerpts included in each title are selected if they contribute valuable, long-range ideas to the overall debate. And wherever possible, current information is enhanced with historical documents and other relevant materials. Thus, while individual titles are current in focus, every effort is made to ensure that they will not become quickly outdated. Books in the *Current Controversies* series will remain important resources for librarians, teachers, and students for many years.

In addition to keeping the titles focused and specific, great care is taken in the editorial format of each book in the series. Book introductions and chapter prefaces are offered to provide background material for readers. Chapters are organized around several key questions that are answered with diverse opinions representing all points on the political spectrum. Materials in each chapter include opinions in which authors clearly disagree as well as alternative opinions in which authors may agree on a broader issue but disagree on the possible solutions. In this way, the content of each volume in *Current Controversies* mirrors the mosaic of opinions encountered in society. Readers will quickly realize that there are many viable answers to these complex issues. By questioning each author's conclusions, students and casual readers can begin to develop the critical thinking skills so important to evaluating opinionated material.

Current Controversies is also ideal for controlled research. Each anthology in the series is composed of primary sources taken from a wide gamut of informational categories including periodicals, newspapers, books, U.S. and foreign government documents, and the publications of private and public organizations. Readers will find factual support for reports, debates, and research papers covering all areas of important issues. In addition, an annotated table of contents, an index, a book and periodical bibliography, and a list of organizations to contact are included in each book to expedite further research.

Perhaps more than ever before in history, people are confronted with diverse and contradictory information. During the Persian Gulf War, for example, the public was not only treated to minute-to-minute coverage of the war, it was also inundated with critiques of the coverage and countless analyses of the factors motivating U.S. involvement. Being able to sort through the plethora of opinions accompanying today's major issues, and to draw one's own conclusions, can be a complicated and frustrating struggle. It is the editors' hope that *Current Controversies* will help readers with this struggle.

Introduction

"Despite the humane goals of animal rights organizations, ... some of these groups are considered by the federal and many state governments to be dangerous domestic terrorists."

Advocacy for animal rights—the idea that animals should not be used or consumed by humans for food, clothing, medical experimentation, or entertainment—is a growing phenomenon, especially in the United States and Europe. In the United States, such groups as People for the Ethical Treatment of Animals (PETA), the Animal Liberation Front (ALF), and the Earth Liberation Front (ELF) work to stop pain and suffering of animals caused by human actions and industries and share the goal of liberating animals from all forms of human exploitation. According to animal rights attorney Dara Lovitz, some of the main targets of animal activists' protests are:

> The agricultural industry, in which farm animals, including cows, pigs, and chickens, are housed in windowless metal warehouses, rotted wire cages, and/or gestation crates; the clothing industry, in which animals like minks, cows, and sheep are skinned alive, castrated without anesthetics, and/or eventually killed by anal or genital electrocution; and the scientific industry, in which animals, including dogs, mice, and monkeys, are subjected to being forced to inhale cigarette smoke, having probes inserted into their heads, and/or being made sick by deadly viruses.

In essence, these groups want to completely abolish the farming of animals for meat, dairy, eggs, and other food products, as well as the production of leather and fur for the clothing industry. They also object to using animals to test drugs, cosmetics, or other products or medical procedures, and they want to ban all forms of hunting, the use of animals for entertainment in circuses and rodeos, and the holding of animals in captivity by zoos and marine parks. Some members of these groups even view pet ownership as a form of animal exploitation. The animal rights position differs from the idea of animal welfare, which seeks to improve conditions for animals while still allowing their use for human benefits. Instead, animal rights advocates believe that animals should not be treated as the property of humans and that animals have just as much of a right to live out their lives freely as people do. Polls say that the animal rights viewpoint is gaining acceptance among the public, due to the efforts of committed animal activists.

Despite the humane goals of animal rights organizations, however, some of these groups are considered by the federal and many state governments to be dangerous domestic terrorists. The U.S. Department of Justice, for example, labels the ALF and ELF as terrorist organizations under the USA PATRIOT Act, the antiterrorism law passed in the wake of the September 11, 2001, terrorist attacks. (USA PATRIOT is an acronym that stands for "Uniting and Strengthening America by Providing Appropriate Tools Required to Intercept and Obstruct Terrorists.") The U.S. Congress in 2006 passed another law, the Animal Enterprise Terrorism Act, specifically to provide the Department of Justice with the authority to apprehend, prosecute, and convict individuals committing "animal enterprise terror." And a number of states have enacted their own laws proscribing animal rights "terrorism."

These government concerns are based on the use of violence by some animal advocates to make their case for animal rights. While PETA has generally sought to avoid violence and instead engages in various nonviolent protests and publicity stunts to promote the cause of animal rights in the media, ALF and ELF have taken more confrontational actions, such as rescues of farm animals or attacks on medical research companies and their employees. Animal activist Daniel Andreas of San Diego, for example, is wanted by the Federal Bureau of Investigation (FBI) because he is believed to have assisted with the bombings of two medical research companies in California in 2003. The FBI has charged Andreas with maliciously damaging and destroying, and attempting to destroy and damage, by means of explosives, buildings and other property. And in the United Kingdom, a group called Stop Huntingdon Animal Cruelty (SHAC) is conducting an international campaign against Huntingdon Life Sciences, one of Europe's largest animal testing laboratories. SHAC has attacked Huntingdon offices, as well as those of other companies that do business with Huntingdon, and has used intimidation, harassment, and violent tactics against Huntingdon employees and their families. The company's managing director, for example, was beaten by three masked assailants swinging baseball bats, and its marketing director was attacked at his home with a chemical that caused him to suffer temporary blindness. This campaign is supported in the United States by ALF, which has been linked with attacks on U.S. companies that are customers or stockholders of Huntingdon. The FBI estimates that ALF and ELF combined have committed hundreds of criminal acts in the United States since 1996, resulting in damages of more than $43 million.

Animal activists and some commentators, however, criticize the federal and state governments for grouping animal lovers and peaceful activists with the terrorists who flew airplanes into the World Trade Center and the Pentagon in 2001. According to this view, the real criminals are not animal activists who engage in minor acts of property damage, harassment, and nonlethal violence, but rather those who murder, mutilate, and torture voiceless animals every day for the sake of profit. Legal commentators have also pointed out that a broad definition of terrorism in federal or state law can threaten Americans' civil liberties, including the First Amendment right of free speech. By defining attacks on mere property as terrorism, and in some cases using vague language that prohibits all actions that "disrupt" businesses, antiterrorism laws could be applied to legitimate, nonviolent protests that have historically been considered protected speech under the U.S. Constitution.

The debate over animal rights is likely to continue, given the passionate views of activists, the growing public concern for the welfare of farm and test animals, and the government's interest in preventing domestic extremism. The various contributors to *Rights of Animals: Current Controversies* provide additional insight into the ethics and reality of this compelling issue.

CHAPTER 1

Should Animals Have Rights?

Chapter Overview:
The Animal Rights Debate

Joseph Lubinski

Joseph Lubinski is a graduate of the University of Denver and the University of Colorado School of Law. He is currently an associate at the Denver-based law firm of Ballard Spahr Andrews & Ingersoll, LLP.

Whether at home, on the farm, or at the dinner table, animals play an important role in everyday human life. They serve as companions, a source of livelihood, entertainment, inspiration, and of course food and clothing to people all across the world. Yet animals can and do exist independent from people and, as living beings, they arguably have interests separate and apart from their utility to humanity. As such, society is increasingly faced with legal, economic, and ethical dilemmas about the proper place for animals and the extent to which their interests should be respected, even when those interests conflict with what is best for humans. Recognition of these issues has given rise to a new social movement, one that seeks to attain increased legal protections, and even the recognition of actual "rights", for nonhuman animals. Not surprisingly, this push has met with a considerable amount of criticism and ridicule from those who believe that the cost of animal rights specifically, and increased protections more generally, is a corresponding reduction in human freedom. . . .

Animals in Society Today

The prevalence of animals in society makes a detailed discussion of their importance unnecessary. Nonetheless, it is worth briefly summarizing some of the figures to emphasize just how important animals are to American society and the

Joseph Lubinski, "Introduction to Animal Rights," Animal Legal and Historical Center, 2004. Reproduced by permission. www.animallaw.info/articles/ddusjlubinski2002.htm.

economy. According to the Census of Agriculture, in 1997 there were 98,989,244 cattle and calves used in United States agriculture, 61,206,236 hogs and pigs, 7,821,885 sheep and lambs, and over 7 billion chickens used for egg and meat production. In that same year the total value of all cattle and poultry was nearly $100 billion.

Over 18 million animals are used in research and experimentation in the United States.

Agriculture is but the tip of the proverbial iceberg, however. Anyone who questions the bond between people and their pets need only look at statistics detailing the number of people who celebrate their pet's birthdays, stay home from work when a pet is sick, or greet their pet first when coming home in the evening. As detailed by the American Veterinary Medical Association:

> Veterinarians in private clinical practice are responsible for the health of approximately 53 million dogs [and] 59 million cats. Bird ownership has risen over the past 5 years from 11 million in 1991 to approximately 13 million birds. The number of pleasure horses in the U.S. is about 4.0 million. Other pets such as rabbits, ferrets, guinea pigs, hamsters, gerbils, other rodents, turtles, snakes, lizards, other reptiles and many other animals primarily kept as companion animals. Rabbits and ferrets are owned by 2.3% of households in the U.S. with a total population of 5.7 million; 4.8 million rodents are owned by 2.3% of households and 1.5% of households own 3.5 million reptiles. The fish population is estimated at 55.6 million owned by 6.3% of households

Of course, animals can also be found in the laboratory. A wide variety of species are used in research and experimentation. In fact, over 18 million animals are used in research and experimentation in the United States. . . .

The Views of Animal Advocates

Even within the animal protection movement there is disagreement about the goals that should be sought on behalf of other species. Roughly, there are three competing philosophies: traditional welfare theory, animal rights, and "new welfarism." While each seeks to advance the protections afforded animals under the law, they differ in approach and the ends sought to be attained.

[Animal] welfare advocates seek a benevolent dominion over animals that expressly reaffirms humanity's superiority to other species.

Briefly, one might understand welfare and rights to lie at opposite ends of the protectionist spectrum. Animal welfare advocates support the types of reforms long sought on behalf of animals—increased penalties for unjustifiable harsh treatment, in other words. Welfarists accept the legal status of other species as property, even condoning such a classification. Moreover, they acknowledge that animals always will be, and perhaps to some extent should be, used as resources for humanity. The limit, however, is that animals should not suffer unnecessarily at the hands of people. In short, then, welfare advocates seek a benevolent dominion over animals that expressly reaffirms humanity's superiority to other species.

Many of the contemporary gains made on behalf of animals are welfare-based in nature. For instance, at the federal level, statutes such as the Animal Welfare Act and the Humane Slaughter Method Act seek to ensure that animals used in industry are treated appropriately. State anti-cruelty laws aim to proscribe the mistreatment of animals by private citizens, in other words setting the bounds for the treatment of dogs, cats, birds, and the like.

Take note that the goal is to regulate unnecessary pain and suffering, not all suffering. This means that it is all right to eat animals, to use them for some experimentation, to domesticate them, and in some circumstances to kill them. Moreover, the effectiveness of welfarism in protecting animals depends on how broadly or narrowly a society chooses to define "unnecessary" in various circumstances. Thus, welfarists seek no fundamental change in the legal order, only increased protections within the current regime.

[Animal] rights advocates do not accept the property status of animals nor the wisdom of subjecting them to human domination.

On the other end of the protectionist spectrum lie animal rights advocates. Rights advocates seek to first change the fundamental legal status of animals away from mere property towards something closer to personhood. Such a change would open the door to more expansive reforms down the line. At base, rights advocates believe that all animals, human and otherwise, possess some inalienable rights that deserve recognition and protection. To the law, these might be characterized as fundamental rights that must never be abridged except in the most dire of circumstances. The number and scope of such rights do not come in one size, but rather are unique based on the intellect and capabilities of each species. Therefore, rights advocates do not seek to equate human rights with those of animals, but rather recognition that some animal rights do exist.

No Status as Property

Thus, rights advocates do not accept the property status of animals nor the wisdom of subjecting them to human domination. Animal experimentation in laboratories, even if helpful to humans, is [in their view] unjustified. Factory farming, and perhaps the meat industry itself, is immoral. Indeed, one must be careful not to eat produce sprayed with pesticides that cost insects their lives. Even the concept of pet ownership is suspect under the rights framework. Acceptance of this rights position requires a rejection of American law as it currently stands.

Many religions teach that it is the existence of a soul that makes human life so sacred and only humans possess souls.

Such seemingly radical reforms make rights advances hard to come by. As such, those dissatisfied by both extremes may look for an alternative approach. Lying between the rights and welfare points on the spectrum exists what Professor [Gary] Francione [an American legal scholar] calls "new welfarism." At its most fundamental level, new welfarism represents a sort of compromise between rights and welfare whereby animal advocates accept traditional welfare gains in the hope that they will eventually amount to a recognition of animal rights. The new welfarist is identified by several characteristics. First, she rejects the notion that animals are merely tools for humanity. Second, is a rejection of the traditional animal rights framework as too radical to effect real change. Third, the strategies they instead employ tend to mimic those of traditional welfare-based groups. To rights activists, the effect of such an approach is to substantially reinforce the human dominance over animals they claim to reject. In so doing, they perceive [as Francione states] no "moral or logical inconsistency in promoting measures that explicitly endorse or reinforce [a] . . . view of animals [as instrumentalities of humanity] and at the same time articulating a long-term philosophy of animal rights." In a more sympathetic light, new welfarists might be thought of as realistic rights advocates—taking what they can get now and hoping for more expansive reforms in the future.

The Anti–Animal Rights Position

Animal rights opponents object to both the concept of rights for nonhumans and its practical implications. On a philosophical level, animal rights would devalue humans by putting them on par with other, perhaps all other, life on the planet. Even if one were to accept that the differences between people and animals are subtle, it is the accumulation of these differences that makes civilization possible. To equate humans to animals, to really believe we are the same, one must dismiss [as David Schmahmann and Lori Polacheck state:] "innate human characteristics, the ability to express reason, to recognize moral principles, to make subtle distinctions, and to intellectualize." In other words, one must dismiss a lot about humans to equate them with other species. Moreover, such objections do not encompass the many religious objections to animal rights. Many religions teach that it is the existence of a soul that makes human life so sacred and only humans possess souls. Finally, one should not overlook the biblical grant of dominion over animals given to man.

In a similar but distinct vein, rights are something intrinsically unique to humans. Rights are simply a term we attach to the special significance given to human life. The existence of rights, and the extension thereof, is a human debate; one in which, by definition, animals cannot have a voice. This principle has broader implications. Peter Singer is famous for his accusation that humanity is "speciesist," or heavily favors its own kind. Others mean the same thing when they call humans homocentric or narcissistic. They complain people always put people first. But is that so wrong? Why shouldn't a species care most for its own, even if that means exploiting another? Put another way, this is how the animal kingdom works. A mother bear does not care what effect her actions have on the rest of the animals in the forest, only on her cubs. The coyote, when he devours livestock, does not consider the impact such a taking will have on the rancher's livelihood, much less the well-being of the cattle.

Moreover, the rights opponents contend, society always has and still does reject any notion of rights for animals. As Steven Wise, one of the leading animal rights advocates in the country, notes, people have long treated animals as "things." Animals are things, like trees and oil, which we use for our own benefit. This is a reality recognized by the courts. Take for example the United States Supreme Court's opinion in *Church of Lukumi Babalu Aye, Inc. v. City of Hialeah*. In that case, a Florida city passed an ordinance aimed at prohibiting the animal sacrifices performed by members of the Santeria religion. The law was challenged in court on First Amendment free exercise of religion grounds. As part of its defense, the city claimed the law was intended to safeguard animals from unnecessary suffering. The Court rejected this argument almost out of hand, making numerous references to the cruelty humanity inflicts on animals all the time, conduct not regulated by the statute.

Animal advocates, whether noble activists or misguided fanatics, face an uphill battle in winning over society and the legal system.

Few Oppose Animal Welfare

In speaking about the anti–animal *rights* position, it is important to note that many such people do not draw the same distinction between rights and welfare as done by animal advocates. More importantly, few would classify themselves as against true animal welfare—some sort of philosophical position that seeks to inflict truly unnecessary harm on animals. Quite to the contrary, most such people believe instead that there are already adequate animal protection laws on the books and that any additional laws can only be intended by the animal protection movement as a prelude to future more controversial reforms.

The Role of Economics

Apart from competing philosophies, there are external forces at work that discourage greater gains for animal protection. Money as they say, talks. Animals are, for lack of a better description, big business in America and elsewhere. A look around the average house demonstrates the important role that animals play in the economy. Household use of animal products extends far beyond leather shoes and the food in the refrigerator, however. As Professor Wise points out:

> The blood of a slaughtered cow is used to manufacture plywood adhesives, fertilizer, fire extinguisher foam, and dyes. Her fat helps make plastic, tires, crayons, cosmetics, lubricants, soaps, detergents, cough syrup, contraceptive jellies and creams, ink, shaving cream, fabric softeners, synthetic rubber, jet engine lubricants, textiles, corrosion inhibitors, and metal-machining lubricants. Her collagen is found in pie crusts, yogurts, matches, bank notes, paper, and cardboard glue; her intestines are used in strings for musical instruments and racquets; her bones in charcoal ash for refining sugar, in ceramics, and cleaning and polishing compounds.

The family pet is likely a product of the dog breeding industry. Factory farming techniques helped put meat, cheese, and eggs on the table at a reasonable price. Dog racing, horse racing, and hunting provide both entertainment and income to millions across the country. The list is nearly infinite, but the point is that the current status and treatment of animals is deeply interwoven into the American capitalist system. It must therefore be considered what effect a change to the legal status of animals would have on the national labor market and cost of goods. Any change to the law that significantly alters the relationship between humanity and this lucrative property line would have deep repercussions within the economy.

International Economic Impact

International economics also discourage significant changes to the legal status of animals. With increasing globalization and the emergence of a worldwide marketplace has also come the proverbial "race to the bottom" in regulatory practices. Thus, as a result of the comprehensive American laws meant to provide protection to the average employee, companies have moved many jobs to other countries where there is less workplace regulation and the cost of labor is far less expensive. Similarly, it seems likely that if the United States were to create more substantive protections for animals, thereby increasing the cost of delivering animal products to consumers, corporate farms and ranches would simply move their facilities to another country where animals do not enjoy similar protections. In so doing, they would be able to provide a comparable product at prices far less than could domestic producers who would in turn be forced out of business. The result, though "feel good" for animal advocates, might net only negligible gains for animal welfare. In a world, then, where anything that has to be there overnight can be, animal advocates must propose not only legislation in their home [countries], but also seek international change as well.

Culture and Tradition

Perhaps more important than money, human culture encourages a continuance of society's current treatment of animals. The use, and some might say abuse, of animals is well established. While one might feel sympathy for the needs of his or her own dog or perhaps even the stray on the corner, that same concern probably does not extend to the turkey at Thanksgiving. Indeed, the recognition of animal rights might well mean the end of many cherished items and traditions, such as leather seats, shoes, and baseballs.

Similarly, there are hobbies and sports dependent on the treatment of animals as something less than legal individuals. Animal rights opponents quite rightly point out that both hunting and fishing might well come to an end if animal protections are allowed to advance too far, not to mention other sports such as dog and horse racing. Moreover, people have become used to viewing animals as things, as exhibits at the zoo or entertainers in the circus ring. Indeed, these human perceptions and customs are so self-evident they need no further elaboration. Taken as a whole, then, one sees that animal advocates, whether noble activists or misguided fanatics, face an uphill battle in winning over society and the legal system.

Animals Should Have a Right Not to Be Exploited

Tom Regan

Tom Regan is an advocate for animal rights and the author of the books The Case for Animal Rights *and* The Struggle for Animal Rights. *He is also emeritus professor of philosophy at North Carolina State University in Raleigh, North Carolina.*

I regard myself as an advocate of animal rights—as part of the animal rights movement. That movement, as I conceive it, is committed to a number of goals, including the total abolition of the use of Animal Research; the total dissolution of commercial animal agriculture; and the total elimination of commercial and sport hunting and trapping.

The Whole System Is Wrong

There are, I know, those who profess to believe in animal rights but do not avow these goals. Factory farming, they say, is wrong—it violates animals' rights—but traditional animal agriculture is all right. Toxicity tests of cosmetics on animals violates their rights, but important medical research—cancer research, for example—does not. The clubbing of seals is abhorrent, but not the harvesting of adult seals. I used to think I understood this reasoning. Not anymore. You don't change unjust institutions by tidying them up.

What's wrong—fundamentally wrong—with the way animals are treated isn't the details that vary from case to case. It's the whole system. The forlornness of the veal calf is pathetic, heart-wrenching; the pulsing pain of the chimp with electrodes planted deep in her brain is repulsive; the slow, torturous death of the raccoon caught in the leghold trap is ago-

Tom Regan, "The Case for Animal Rights," *TomRegan-AnimalRights.com*, reproduced by permission of Blackwell Publishers. www.tomregan-animalrights.com/regan_rites.html.

nizing. But what is wrong isn't the pain, isn't the suffering, isn't the deprivation. These compound what's wrong. Sometimes—often—they make it much, much worse. But they are not the fundamental wrong.

The fundamental wrong is the system that allows us to view animals as our resources, here for us—to be eaten, or surgically manipulated, or exploited for sport or money. Once we accept this view of animals—as our resources—the rest is as predictable as it is regrettable. Why worry about their loneliness, their pain, their death? Since animals exist for us, to benefit us in one way or another, what harms them really doesn't matter—or matters only if it starts to bother us, makes us feel a trifle uneasy when we eat our veal escallop, for example. So, yes, let us get veal calves out of solitary confinement, give them more space, a little straw, a few companions. But let us keep our veal escallop.

But a little straw, more space and a few companions won't eliminate—won't even touch—the basic wrong that attaches to our viewing and treating animals as our resources. A veal calf killed to be eaten after living in close confinement is viewed and treated in this way: but so, too, is another who is raised (as they say) "more humanely." To right the wrong of our treatment of farm animals requires more than making rearing methods "more humane"; it requires the total dissolution of commercial animal agriculture.

Enough people ... must believe in change—must want it—before we will have laws that protect the rights of animals.

How we do this, whether we do it or, as in the case of Animal Research, whether and how we abolish their use— these are to a large extent political questions. People must change their beliefs before they change their habits. Enough people, especially those elected to public office, must believe in change—must want it—before we will have laws that protect the rights of animals. This process of change is very complicated, very demanding, very exhausting, calling for the efforts of many hands in education, publicity, political organization and activity, down to the licking of envelopes and stamps. As a trained and practicing philosopher, the sort of contribution I can make is limited but, I like to think, important. The currency of philosophy is ideas—their meaning and rational foundation—not the nuts and bolts of the legislative process, say, or the mechanics of community organization. That's what I have been exploring over the past ten years or so in my essays and talks and, most recently, in my books, *The Case for Animal Rights* and *The Struggle for Animal Rights*. I believe the major conclusions I reach in the books are true because they are supported by the weight of the best arguments. I believe the idea of animal rights has reason, not just emotion, on its side. . . .

The Animal Rights View

The [animal] rights view, I believe, is rationally the most satisfactory moral theory. It surpasses all other theories in the degree to which it illuminates and explains the foundations of our duties to one another—the domain of human morality. On this score it has the best reasons, the best arguments, on its side. Of course, if it were possible to show that only human beings are included within its scope, then a person like myself, who believes in animal rights, would be obliged to look elsewhere.

But attempts to limit its scope to humans only can be shown to be rationally defective. Animals, it is true, lack many of the abilities humans possess. They can't read, do higher mathematics, build a bookcase or make baba ghanoush. Neither can many human beings, however, and yet we don't (and shouldn't) say that they (these humans) therefore have less inherent value, less of a right to be treated with respect, than do others. It is the similarities between those human beings who most clearly, most non-controversially have such value (the people reading this, for example), not our differences, that matter most. And the really crucial, the basic similarity is simply this: we are each of us the experiencing subject of a life, a conscious creature having an individual welfare that has importance to us whatever our usefulness to others.

[Animals] must be viewed as the experiencing subjects of a life, with inherent value of their own.

We want and prefer things, believe and feel things, recall and expect things. And all these dimensions of our life, including our pleasure and pain, our enjoyment and suffering, our satisfaction and frustration, our continued existence or our untimely death—all make a difference to the quality of our life as lived, as experienced, by us as individuals. As the same is true of those animals that concern us (the ones who are eaten and trapped, for example), they too must be viewed as the experiencing subjects of a life, with inherent value of their own.

The Inherent Value of Animals

Some . . . resist the idea that animals have inherent value. "Only humans have such value," they profess. How might this narrow view be defended? Shall we say that only humans have the requisite intelligence, or autonomy, or reason? But there are many, many humans who fail to meet these standards and yet are reasonably viewed as having value above and beyond their usefulness to others. Shall we claim that only humans belong to the right species, the species *Homo sapiens*? But this is blatant speciesism. Will it be said, then, that all—and only—humans have immortal souls? Then our opponents have their work cut out for them. I am myself not ill-disposed to the proposition that there are immortal souls. Personally, I profoundly hope I have one. But I would not want to rest my position on a controversial ethical issue on the even more controversial question about who or what has an immortal soul. That is to dig one's hole deeper, not to climb out. Rationally, it is better to resolve moral issues without making more controversial assumptions than are needed. The question of who has inherent value is such a question, one that is resolved more rationally without the introduction of the idea of immortal souls than by its use.

Well, perhaps some will say that animals have some inherent value, only less than we have. Once again, however, attempts to defend this view can be shown to lack rational justification. What could be the basis of our having more inherent value than animals? Their lack of reason, or autonomy, or intellect? Only if we are willing to make the same judgement in the case of humans who are similarly deficient. But it is not true that such humans—the retarded child, for example, or the mentally deranged—have less inherent value than you or I. Neither, then, can we rationally sustain the view that animals . . . have less inherent value. All who have inherent value have it equally, whether they be human animals or not.

Reason compels us to recognize the equal inherent value of . . . animals and, with this, their equal right to be treated with respect.

Inherent value, then, belongs equally to those who are the experiencing subjects of a life. Whether it belongs to others—to rocks and rivers, trees and glaciers, for example—we do not know. But we do not need to know, for example, how many people are eligible to vote in the next presidential election before we can know whether I am. Similarly, we do not need to know how many individuals have inherent value before we can know that some do. When it comes to the case for animal rights, then, what we need to know is whether the animals that, in our culture, are routinely eaten, hunted and used in our laboratories, for example, are like us in being subjects of a life. And we do know this. We do know that many—literally, billions—of these animals are the subjects of a life in the sense explained and so have inherent value if we do. And since, in order to arrive at the best theory of our duties to one another, we must recognize our equal inherent value as individuals, reason—not sentiment, not emotion—reason compels us to recognize the equal inherent value of these animals and, with this, their equal right to be treated with respect. . . .

Implications of Animal Rights

I must, in closing [my argument for the case for animal rights] limit myself to four final points. The first is how the theory that underlies the case for animal rights shows that the animal rights movement is a part of, not antagonistic to, the human rights movement. The theory that rationally grounds the rights of animals also grounds the rights of humans.

Secondly, having set out the broad outlines of the rights view, I can now say why its implications for farming and science, among other fields, are both clear and uncompromising. In the case of the use of Animal Research, the rights view is categorically abolitionist. Lab animals are not our tasters; we are not their kings. Because these animals are treated routinely, systematically as if their value were reducible to their usefulness to others, they are routinely, systematically treated with a lack of respect, and thus are their rights routinely, systematically violated. This is just as true when they are used in trivial, duplicative, unnecessary or unwise research as it is when they are used in studies that hold out real promise for human beings.

We can't justify harming or killing a human being . . . just for these sorts of reasons. Neither can we do so even in the case of so "lowly" a creature as a laboratory rat. It is not just refinement or reduction that is called for, not just larger, cleaner cages, not just more generous use of anesthetic or the elimination of multiple surgery, not just tidying up the system. It is complete replacement. The best we can do when it comes to using Animal Research is—not to use them. That is where our duty lies, according to the rights view.

Morality requires nothing less than the total elimination of hunting and trapping for commercial and sporting ends.

As for commercial animal agriculture, the rights view takes a similar abolitionist position. The fundamental moral wrong here is not that animals are kept in stressful close confinement or in isolation, or that their pain and suffering, their needs and preferences are ignored or discounted. All these are wrong, of course, but they are not the fundamental wrong. They are symptoms and effects of the deeper, systematic wrong that allows these animals to be viewed and treated as lacking independent value, as resources for us—as, indeed, a renewable resource. Giving farm animals more space, more natural environments, more companions does not right the fundamental wrong in their case. Nothing less than the total dissolution of commercial animal agriculture will do this, just as, for similar reasons I won't develop at length here, morality requires nothing less than the total elimination of hunting and trapping for commercial and sporting ends. The rights view's implications, then, as I have said, are clear and uncompromising.

My last two points are about philosophy, my profession. It is, most obviously, no substitute for political action. The words I have written here and in other places by themselves don't change a thing. It is what we do with the thoughts that the words express—our acts, our deeds—that changes things. All that philosophy can do, and all I have attempted, is to offer a vision of what our needs should aim at. And the why. But not the how.

Need for Disciplined Passion

Finally, I am reminded of my thoughtful critic, the one who chastised me for being too cerebral. I am also reminded, however, of the image another friend once set before me—the image of the ballerina as expressive of disciplined passion. Long hours of sweat and toil, of loneliness and practice, of doubt and fatigue: those are the disciplines of her craft. But the passion is there, too: the fierce drive to. excel, to speak through her body, to do it right, to pierce our minds. That is the image of philosophy I would leave with you, not "too cerebral" but disciplined passion. Of the discipline enough has been seen. As for the passion: there are times, and these not infrequent, when tears come to my eyes when I see, or read, or hear of the wretched plight of animals in the hands of humans. Their pain, their suffering, their loneliness, their innocence, their death. Anger. Rage. Pity. Sorrow. Disgust. The whole creation groans under the weight of the evil we humans visit upon these mute, powerless creatures. It is our hearts, not just our heads, that call for an end to it all, that demand of us that we overcome, for them, the habits and forces behind their systematic oppression. All great movements, it is written, go through three stages: ridicule, discussion, adoption. It is the realization of this third stage, adoption, that requires both our passion and our discipline, our hearts and our heads. The fate of animals is in our hands. God grant we are equal to the task.

Differences Between Animals and Humans Do Not Justify Denying Animals Basic Rights

Lesli Bisgould

Lesli Bisgould is a Toronto lawyer with a special interest in animal rights.

I look a lot like corned beef on the inside. This, among many impressions made on me by Body Worlds 2—the Anatomical Exhibition of Real Human Bodies [recently on display] at the Ontario Science Centre—was the most overwhelming. It includes whole human bodies, posed, sliced and displayed so as to reveal bones, muscles, tendons, nerves, blood vessels, internal organs, skin, eyes, even hair. They are preserved using a method called "plastination."

Moving among the carcasses, or "plastinates," as the audio recording calls them, the viewer comes face to face with her own inner workings. Some find it fascinating, others discomfiting—mortality sure seems real when you get so close and personal—but what struck me most was the similarity of our flesh to what most people think of as food.

We are used to thinking about animals as dead meat. In fact, the most intimate experience most of us have with animals begins when they are dead and we eat them. So we do not flinch when they are referred to as "carcasses," "specimens" and "displays." But we are not accustomed to seeing ourselves so exposed and dead, nor to confronting our inner similarities.

Of course, in reality, we are all animals. There is no magical line dividing "us" from "them"; so categorically, even if it's convenient for us to pretend otherwise come dinnertime. In the many decades since Darwin first said "evolution," he and the scientists who followed have made quite a clear case about the similarities between animals, and about the differences, which Darwin knew to be in degree, not in kind.

We have learned that the real world is made up of individuals who are more or less closely related to one another by virtue of our descent from a common ancestor. When we say "species" we are really just trying to give some order to the otherwise chaotic and splendid variety that is nature. It also turns out to be a handy tool of discrimination.

Differences Are Irrelevant to Rights

Once we claimed an entitlement to eat and otherwise use animals for our own purposes because we thought they were somehow deficient and less worthy—they can't think or reason, they don't feel or communicate—but we have since learned that we were wrong. Today we know that animals are complex creatures, with their own intelligence, developed over evolutionary time, to enable each one to succeed in her particular environment. An emperor penguin can't do calculus and I can't protect an egg on my feet through an Antarctic winter. What was really deficient was our own ability to understand them.

There are surely differences between mice and men, as there are between carp and gorillas and kittens and giraffes. There are differences between people, too. When we speak of equality in the human world, it is never to imply that we are all actually equal. We have different builds and appearances and different abilities. Some are better at math than others, some are better singers, some are better hockey players. But we have decided that these differences, while they may be relevant in determining who is entitled to an Olympic medal, for example, are not morally relevant when it comes to deciding who is entitled to basic, fundamental rights. Like the right to live and not have one's interests sacrificed in the name of the interests of somebody else.

When advocating for animal rights, nobody means the right to vote or to a full year of maternity benefits. It is not human rights for animals. It is, rather, the logical extension of an argument we have already accepted among our own kind, at least ostensibly: We ought not to discriminate against one another based on irrelevant grounds. Animal-rights advocates ask what morally relevant differences there are between humans and the many thousands of other animals with whom we comprise the animal kingdom that make it all right for us to harm them in ways that we would never tolerate against one of our own kind, no matter how diseased or vicious.

Why is it all right to elevate one animal to master and reduce all the others to their edible parts?

We annually hurt hundreds of millions of animals in this country in lawful, institutionalized and profitable ways. We prohibit causing them "unnecessary" pain and suffering, meaning we have written right into our laws permission to hurt them, any of them, when we think it is necessary for our own purposes. And so it is "necessary" to mutilate, electrocute, burn, confine, isolate, starve and terrify individuals and we do so regularly in the name of agriculture, science, fashion, entertainment and other industries. But unless we are willing to accept "because we can" as a valid moral theory, we must face the fact that, at least since Darwin, the justification for our behaviour has lost its factual premise.

We are all meat, and all meat is carrion, cooked or otherwise. Why is it all right to elevate one animal to master and reduce all the others to their edible parts? Body Parts 2 makes us confront that question and perhaps it makes us uncomfortable enough to try to come up with an honest answer.

Whether a Right or Not, Animals Should Be Treated Morally

Sam Vaknin

Sam Vaknin is an author and columnist for a number of online publications.

"Animal rights" is a catchphrase akin to "human rights." It involves, however, a few pitfalls. First, animals exist only as a concept. Otherwise, they are cuddly cats, curly dogs, cute monkeys. A rat and a puppy are both animals but our emotional reaction to them is so different that we cannot really lump them together. Moreover: what rights are we talking about? The right to life? The right to be free of pain? The right to food? Except the right to free speech, all other rights could be applied to animals.

Difficulties

Law professor Steven Wise argues in his book, *Drawing the Line: Science and the Case for Animal Rights*, for the extension to animals of legal rights accorded to infants. Many animal species exhibit awareness, cognizance and communication skills typical of human toddlers and of humans with arrested development. Yet, the latter enjoy rights denied the former.

According to Wise, there are four categories of practical autonomy—a legal standard for granting "personhood" and the rights it entails. Practical autonomy involves the ability to be desirous, to intend to fulfill and pursue one's desires, a sense of self-awareness, and self-sufficiency. Most animals, says Wise, qualify. This may be going too far. It is easier to justify the moral rights of animals than their legal rights.

Sam Vaknin, "The Rights of Animals," Animal Liberation Front Web site, October 9, 2006. Reproduced by permission. www.animalliberationfront.com/Philosophy/TheRightsofAnimals.htm.

But when we say "animals," what we really mean is non-human organisms. This is such a wide definition that it easily pertains to extraterrestrial aliens. Will we witness an Alien Rights movement soon? Unlikely. Thus, we are forced to narrow our field of enquiry to non-human organisms reminiscent of humans, the ones that provoke in us empathy.

Even this is way too fuzzy. Many people love snakes, for instance, and deeply empathize with them. Could we accept the assertion (avidly propounded by these people) that snakes ought to have rights, or should we consider only organisms with extremities and the ability to feel pain?

Views of Philosophers

Historically, philosophers like [Immanuel] Kant (and [René] Descartes, [Nicolas] Malebranche, and [Thomas] Aquinas) rejected the idea of animal rights. They regarded animals as the organic equivalents of machines, driven by coarse instincts, unable to experience pain (though their behavior sometimes deceives us into erroneously believing that they do).

Historically, philosophers . . . rejected the idea of animal rights.

Thus, any ethical obligation that we have towards animals is a derivative of our primary obligation towards our fellow humans (the only ones possessed of moral significance). These are called the theories of indirect moral obligations. Thus, it is wrong to torture animals only because it desensitizes us to human suffering and makes us more prone to using violence on humans. Malebranche augmented this line of thinking by "proving" that animals cannot suffer pain because they are not descended from Adam. Pain and suffering, as we all know, are the exclusive outcomes of Adam's sins.

The Problem of Human Empathy

Kant and Malebranche may have been wrong. Animals may be able to suffer and agonize. But how can we tell whether another Being is truly suffering pain or not? Through empathy. We postulate that—since that Being resembles us—it must have the same experiences and, therefore, it deserves our pity.

Yet, the principle of resemblance has many drawbacks.

One, it leads to moral relativism. Consider this maxim from the Jewish Talmud: "Do not do unto thy friend that which you hate." An analysis of this sentence renders it less altruistic than it appears. We are encouraged to refrain from doing only those things that *we* find hateful. This is the quiddity of moral relativism.

The saying implies that it is the individual who is the source of moral authority. Each and every one of us is allowed to spin his own moral system, independent of others. The Talmudic dictum establishes a privileged moral club ... comprised of oneself and one's friend(s). One is encouraged not to visit evil upon one's friends, all others seemingly excluded. Even the broadest interpretation of the word "friend" could only read: "someone like you" and substantially excludes strangers.

Two, similarity is a structural, not an essential, trait. Empathy as a differentiating principle is structural: if X looks like me and behaves like me, then he is privileged. Moreover, similarity is not necessarily identity. Monkeys, dogs and dolphins are very much like us, both structurally and behaviorally. Even according to Wise, it is quantity (the degree of observed resemblance), not quality (identity, essence), that is used in determining whether an animal is worthy of holding rights, whether it is a morally significant person. The degree of figurative and functional likenesses decide whether one deserves to live, pain-free and happy.

The quantitative test includes the ability to communicate (manipulate vocal-verbal-written symbols within structured symbol systems). Yet, we ignore the fact that using the same symbols does not guarantee that we attach to them the same cognitive interpretations and the same emotional resonance ("private languages"). The same words, or symbols, often have different meanings.

That another organism looks like us, behaves like us and communicates like us is no guarantee that it is—in its essence—like us.

Meaning is dependent upon historical, cultural, and personal contexts. There is no telling whether two people mean the same things when they say "red," or "sad," or "I," or "love." That another organism looks like us, behaves like us and communicates like us is no guarantee that it is—in its essence—like us. This is the subject of the famous Turing Test: there is no effective way to distinguish a machine from a human when we rely exclusively on symbol manipulation.

The Subjective Nature of Pain

Consider pain once more. To say that something does not experience pain cannot be rigorously defended. Pain is a subjective experience. There is no way to prove or to disprove that someone is or is not in pain. Here, we can rely only on the subject's reports. Moreover, even if we were to have an analgometer (pain gauge), there would have been no way to show that the phenomenon that activates the meter is one and the same for all subjects, subjectively, i.e., that it is experienced in the same way by all the subjects examined.

Even more basic questions regarding pain are impossible to answer: What is the connection between the piercing needle and the pain reported and between these two and electrochemical patterns of activity in the brain? A correlation between these three phenomena can be established, but not their identity or the existence of a causative process. We cannot prove that the waves in the subject's brain when he reports pain, *are* that pain. Nor can we show that they caused the pain, or that the pain caused them.

It is also not clear whether our moral precepts are conditioned on the objective existence of pain, on the reported existence of pain, on the purported existence of pain (whether experienced or not, whether reported or not), or on some independent laws.

If it were painless, would it be moral to torture someone? Is the very act of sticking needles into someone immoral, or is it immoral because of the pain it causes, or is supposed to inflict? Are all three components (needle sticking, a sensation of pain, brain activity) morally equivalent? If so, is it as immoral to merely generate the same patterns of brain activity, without inducing any sensation of pain and without sticking needles in the subject?

If these three phenomena are not morally equivalent, why aren't they? They are, after all, different facets of the very same pain, [so] shouldn't we condemn all of them equally? Or should one aspect of pain (the subject's report of pain) be accorded a privileged treatment and status?

Yet, the subject's report is the weakest proof of pain! It cannot be verified. And if we cling to this descriptive-behavioral-phenomenological definition of pain then animals qualify as well. They also exhibit all the behaviors normally ascribed to humans in pain and they report feeling pain (though they do tend to use a more limited and non-verbal vocabulary).

Pain is, therefore, a value judgment and the reaction to it is culturally dependent. In some cases, pain is perceived as positive and is sought. In the Aztec cultures, being chosen to be sacrificed to the Gods was a high honor. How would we judge animal rights in such historical and cultural contexts? Are there any "universal" values or does it all really depend on interpretation?

If we, humans, cannot separate the objective from the subjective and the cultural, what gives us the right or ability to decide for other organisms? We have no way of knowing whether pigs suffer pain. We cannot decide right and wrong, good and evil for those with whom we can communicate, let alone for organisms with which we fall to do even this.

False Distinctions

Is it generally immoral to kill, to torture, to pain? The answer seems obvious and it automatically applies to animals. Is it generally immoral to destroy? Yes, it is and this answer pertains to the inanimate as well. There are exceptions: it is permissible to kill and to inflict pain in order to prevent a (quantitatively or qualitatively) greater evil, to protect life, and when no reasonable and feasible alternative is available.

Ever-escalating cruelty towards other species will not establish our genetic supremacy—merely our moral inferiority.

The chain of food in nature is morally neutral and so are death and disease. Any act which is intended to sustain life of a higher order ... is morally positive or, at least, neutral. Nature decreed so. Animals do it to other animals, though, admittedly, they optimize their consumption and avoid waste and unnecessary pain. Waste and pain are morally wrong. This is not a question of hierarchy of more or less important Beings (an outcome of the fallacy of anthropomorphizing Nature).

The distinction between what is (essentially) us, and what just looks and behaves like us, is false, superfluous and superficial. Sociobiology is already blurring these lines. Quantum Mechanics has taught us that we can say nothing about what the world really is. If things look the same and behave the same, we better assume that they are the same.

The attempt to claim that moral responsibility is reserved to the human species is self defeating. If it is so, then we definitely have a moral obligation towards the weaker and meeker. If it isn't, what right do we have to decide who shall live and who shall die (in pain)? The increasingly shaky "fact" that species do not interbreed "proves" that species are distinct, say some. But who can deny that we share most of our genetic material with the fly and the mouse? We are not as dissimilar as we wish we were. And ever-escalating cruelty towards other species will not establish our genetic supremacy—merely our moral inferiority.

Animals Have Rich Emotional Lives and Consciousness

Ross Robertson

Ross Robertson is associate editor of What Is Enlightenment? *a magazine devoted to spiritual, cultural, and philosophical issues.*

Oftentimes during her lectures and travels, [primatologist Jane] Goodall tells the story of a man named Rick Swope who risked his life to save a chimpanzee named Jo-Jo from drowning in the newly constructed moat surrounding his enclosure at the Detroit Zoo. Among this particular posse of Michigan chimps, Jo-Jo was the head honcho, but when a younger and stronger alpha-wannabe threw down the gauntlet one day and attacked him, Jo-Jo ran, wisely or not so wisely, over the safety barrier and into the water. Chimps can't swim, which is why zoos build moats around them in the first place; chimps are also very dangerous, which is why the zookeeper on duty that day made no attempt to rescue Jo-Jo when he panicked and sank like a stone. Against the keeper's dire warnings, and much to the distress of his wife and kids, Swope jumped in and lifted the 130-pound ape as well as he could up the embankment. "I looked into his eyes," he said later. "It was like looking into the eyes of a man. And the message was: Won't *anybody* help me?"

What was it in Jo-Jo's eyes that made Swope keep himself in jeopardy (three angry males were charging down the bank toward him) in order to support the stunned and waterlogged chimpanzee until he could finally grab a tuft of grass and pull himself to safety? Are the eyes, as the saying goes, really windows to the soul? I can still remember the day when, after an embarrassingly great many years of unsuccessful fishing trips with the Boy Scouts, I finally caught my first fish. As I tried,

Ross Robertson, "Do Animals Have Souls?" *What Is Enlightenment?*, March–May, 2006. Reproduced by permission. www.wie.org/j32/animal-souls.asp.

also unsuccessfully, to extract the hook from its mouth and throw it back, I gazed into its eyes and saw something I thought was sadness. It was hard not to flinch away from that dying look, in which I could see my own carelessness nakedly reflected, but somehow I felt honor-bound not to disturb this intimate channel that, for a brief moment at least, had been opened up between us.

I made other efforts at "interspecies communication" when I was a kid, walking through the woods with my Audubon bird call and mimicking the chirps and trills I heard up above. And though I have no evidence of any definitive success, my crude attempts at avian language were nevertheless a kind of animal soul music, at least in my own mind—a curious call to the nonhuman world in search of the echo of consciousness returning back to me. Who, or what, I wanted to know, was out there listening?

Jamming with Whales

Guitarist Jim Nollman must have been wondering something similar when he anchored his boat off the coast of Vancouver Island, dropped a submersible speaker overboard, plugged in, and tried to get the dolphins and killer whales to jam with him. From recordings he's made using underwater microphones to capture their hornlike whistles and songs (Nollman compares one particularly responsive whale to *Bitches Brew*–era Miles Davis), he appears to have succeeded. Other Western musicians whom Nollman has invited aboard to try out his gear have tended to elicit either clear responses from the whales or no interest at all. A Tibetan lama chanting religious prayers, on the other hand, brought forth a palpable hush. As he intoned his Himalayan melody, the whales approached the speaker quietly and just huddled there, listening.

When pods of killer whales fall strangely silent to eavesdrop on a chanting Buddhist monk, what exactly are they responding to? Is it to the vibrations themselves, sounds and sensations either pleasing or baffling to their ears? Or are they hearing the resonance of something more intangible, some transcendent echo reflected back from deep within them? What is it in us, for that matter, that responds to these things? Is it the soul?

If you still find yourself attached to the belief that animals are hopelessly undeveloped . . . breaking news from the scientific arena is here to recommend otherwise.

Whatever else the soul might be, it seems safe to say that it is part of that dimension of consciousness that makes us most fully human—part of that which makes us thinking, feeling, caring beings. Could the same be true of the animal soul? Not so long ago, noble qualities like reason, emotion, and morality were all thought to be exclusively human traits. But the steady march of science is chipping away at old ideas. In 1960, Goodall observed chimpanzees at Tanzania's Gombe Stream Reserve stripping leaves off twigs and using the sticks to fish termites out of their nests, thereby poking holes in the long-held belief that human beings were the only species to make tools. "Now we must redefine tool," said her mentor Louis Leakey, "redefine man, or accept chimpanzees as humans." Since then, nearly all major arguments for human uniqueness—claims that we alone possess rationality, self-consciousness, culture, empathy, language, morality, etc.—have been increasingly called into question. So if you still find yourself attached to the belief that animals are hopelessly undeveloped—dull of mind, poor of heart, and devoid of soul—breaking news from the scientific arena is here to recommend otherwise.

Mental Abilities of Animals

Let's take *reason,* to start. According to [philosopher René] Descartes, animals were mere machines, while men were machines with minds. Indeed, the bulk of Western thought, from

Plato and Aristotle to Aquinas on up, puts great stock in rationality as *the* basic factor setting human beings apart from the rest of animal kind. And since you can't just walk up to a guinea pig or an anteater and ask it to describe its experience of cognition, it hasn't exactly been easy to test this claim. One way scientists have tried to get at the problem is by searching for evidence of animal deception, a cognitive skill that depends on the ability to recognize that others have thoughts and intentions different from one's own. They've shown that monkeys and baboons can distract each other in order to steal food, sneak around rocks to do things behind each others' backs, and wait until others are distracted (like during fights) to put the moves on receptive females. Just recently, a raven named Hugin passed the deception test as well, fooling a dominant bird into hunting for food where Hugin knew there was none in order to buy himself some time alone where the food really was.

Impressive as Hugin's trick may be, it must look like kids' stuff to one of the most accomplished birds known to science: Alex the parrot. [In the summer of 2005], Alex raised the bar on avian intelligence to new heights by demonstrating a rough understanding of the number zero, a conceptual abstraction never fathomed by even the most learned mathematicians of ancient Greece. How did he do it? Trainer Dr. Irene Pepperberg laid out a tray with four groups of blocks on it—two blue, three green, four yellow, and six orange—and then called out a number of blocks, asking Alex to identify the color of the corresponding group. But for some reason, he refused to cooperate, insisting instead on repeating the word "five" over and over again. When she finally replied "OK, smarty, what color five?" Alex quickly answered "None!" A bird with a brain the size of a walnut had understood the "absence of quantity," something human children don't typically grasp until age three or four.

How did Alex *feel* about his accomplishment? As recently as ten years ago, researchers would have argued over whether it was possible for him to have felt anything at all. But scientists no longer dispute the presence of emotion in birds—or in many other species, for that matter.

Most biologists have accepted that animals have richly varied emotional lives.

African elephants, for instance, "share with us a strong sense of family and death and they feel many of the same emotions," Kenyan conservationist Daphne Sheldrick says. "Each one is . . . a unique individual with its own unique personality. They can be happy or sad, volatile or placid. They display envy, jealousy, throw tantrums and are fiercely competitive, and they can develop hang-ups which are reflected in behaviour. . . . They grieve deeply for lost loved ones, even shedding tears and suffering depression. They have a sense of compassion that projects beyond their own kind and sometimes extends to others in distress." Animal behavior expert Marc Bekoff adds that elephants are known to stand silent guard over stillborn babies for days with their heads and ears sunk low; orphans who witness their mothers' deaths "often wake up screaming." Sea lion mothers howl and cry while killer whales dine on their babies, he says. Dolphins struggle painfully to resuscitate dead infants. Once, he even saw a grieving red fox *bury* the body of another who had been killed by a mountain lion: "She would kick up dirt, stop, look at the carcass, and intentionally kick again. I observed this 'ritual' for about 20 seconds. A few hours later I went to see the carcass, and it was totally buried."

Animal Morality

Now that most biologists have accepted that animals have richly varied emotional lives, a far more radical proposition is taking center stage in current research. Beyond simple raw emotion, some say, animals are displaying the subtler, more complex signs of *moral* sensibility. "There is good evidence that chimpanzees keep track of favors and repay them," writes primatologist Frans de Waal. And it goes both ways, Bekoff tells me: "If you're labeled as a cheater in a pack of wolves or a pack of coyotes or a group of chimpanzees, you're going to have a lot of trouble getting other individuals to interact with you." He calls this "wild justice," and it's not just for primates and canines. Cows hold grudges and nurture friendships too. North African meerkats forfeit their own safety to stay beside wounded family members who would otherwise have to face death alone. Stronger rats sometimes even let the weaker ones win when they play at wrestling. And—remarkable as it sounds—morality in animals also crosses *species* boundaries. "You see animals help each other all the time," Bekoff says. "Dogs and monkeys hug one another, console one another, travel with one another. During the tsunami [of late December 2004], a baby hippopotamus was separated from his family and taken to an animal rescue shelter in Kenya. When he got there, he was adopted by a 130-year-old tortoise, and they've been inseparable ever since." Not long ago, de Waal watched a bonobo named Kuni pick up an injured starling, take it outside, and place it on its feet. When it didn't fly, she helped unfold its wings and then carefully tossed it into the air.

Then there are the stories of animal heroics that involve human beings, some of which have achieved the status of legend. Eleven-year-old Anthony Melton's pet pig, Priscilla, made headlines in 1984 when she dove into a Houston lake to save his life. Swimming out to the boy, who was in over his head and starting to panic, she towed him to shore with her leash. In 1975, a woman shipwrecked off the Philippines was saved by a giant sea turtle that surfaced underneath her and carried her on its back for two full days until rescuers finally arrived.

Once, an elderly Tennessee woman was even rescued by her pet *canary*. Upon seeing her trip and fall unconscious, the bird proceeded to find its way out of her house, which it had never left before. It then traveled the length of several football fields to her niece's nearby home and banged hysterically against the windowpane until she finally got the message and went running to check up on her aunt. The canary promptly collapsed and died from the effort, but the old woman's life was saved.

The question "Do animals have souls?" depends in no small measure on what you think the soul is in the first place.

Of all such tales of interspecies love and bravado, perhaps the most enigmatic and the most miraculous involve dolphins, renowned the world over for keeping unconscious people afloat, shielding swimmers from sharks and sea lions from orcas, guarding pregnant whales while they give birth, and herding beached whales back to open sea. Most incredible of these might be the story of Pelorus Jack, a dolphin famous for guiding steamships through a notoriously treacherous channel off the coast of New Zealand around the turn of the last century. French Pass was known among sailors for claiming vessel after vessel in its swift jaws—that is, until Pelorus Jack came along. For over twenty years, every time a ship approached the mouth of the hazardous strait, he would unfailingly appear, bobbing along the surface to lead it safely through the rocks. On his watch, none ever foundered. Then in 1904, a drunkard on board a ship known as the *Penguin* took a potshot at him and Jack swam away trailing blood. Although he healed a few weeks later and diligently returned to his chosen task, nobody on the *Penguin* ever saw him again; it later ran aground in French Pass, and crew and passengers drowned. . . .

While stories like these may provide the most direct and compelling evidence of soul and soulfulness among our animal kin, the meaning of the word "soul" itself is usually the domain of religion. It's been hotly debated by philosophers and theologians alike down through the centuries, yet the true nature of the soul remains an alluring riddle—hard enough to fathom in human beings, let alone in the rest of the animal kingdom. Still, the question "Do animals have souls?" depends in no small measure on what you think the soul *is* in the first place. . . .

Horizons of Animal Consciousness

Biologist Rupert Sheldrake has spent upwards of fifteen years researching psychic phenomena in animals—things like the impossible synergy of bird flocks wheeling together in unison or the uncanny knack some dogs and cats seem to have for knowing when their owners are coming home. "Unexplained abilities like telepathy," he says, "are widespread in the animal kingdom." . . .

[And] the literature of supernatural experience is positively teeming with the ghosts of pets haunting places and people they knew while they were alive. Once, for example, a veterinarian treating a sick white horse gave its owners some baffling instructions: he told them that for safety's sake, it would be best to separate the ailing animal from the other white horse in its corral. "What other horse?" they asked—and were dumbfounded as the vet went on to describe, in unmistakable detail, a second horse of theirs who had recently died. On another occasion, two young boys were close to drowning in a cold lake near the Austrian border when their father leapt into the water to rescue them. Swimming as fast as he could, he saw that the family dog Fritz had beaten him to the punch and watched as the faithful pet steered his boys back to the beach. The wrinkle: Fritz had been dead for over a year. When they all got to shore, his ghost disappeared, but not before a dozen onlookers had seen him too. . . .

Ultimately, the precise parameters of human uniqueness may be too elusive to pin down, the character of the animal soul too loosely understood to be tied off with any authority. Even so, there's one last question on my mind: What lies in store for the future? Just last September [2005] in the rainforests of the Congo, new types of tool use were observed among wild gorillas. Then in November, researchers in St. Louis made the startling announcement that higher mammals like whales and humans aren't the only ones smart enough to be able to sing—now *mice* have been overheard performing complex (and catchy) ultrasonic love ballads to woo potential mates. And new findings like these seem to be cropping up by the month. Of course, science itself is always progressing, but could these discoveries also suggest that animal consciousness is evolving? If so, are their souls evolving too?

God Did Not Make Animals the Moral Equivalent of Humans

Randy Stiver

Randy Stiver is the pastor of United Church of God congregations in Columbus and Cambridge, Ohio.

If our society were full of common sense, the question of whether animals have rights like people do would never come up—because people would know. Animals are animals and human beings are human beings. That is, if our society had common sense.

The Animal Rights Movement

The modern animal rights movement charts its origin from a book titled *Animal Liberation* printed in 1975. It was written by Australian-born Peter Singer, now a professor of philosophy in America at Princeton University. His book proclaimed that animals, in essence are morally equal to people. . . .

Many initially lump animal rights with animal welfare programs (like animal shelters, etc.)—but these are not the same, as animal rights activists Tom Regan and Gary Francione clarify. "Not only are the philosophies of animal rights and animal welfare separated by irreconcilable differences . . . the enactment of animal welfare measures actually impedes the achievement of animal rights."

The philosophy that spawns the concept of animal rights doesn't come from God. The founder of PETA (People for the Ethical Treatment of Animals), Ingrid Newkirk, made the now-famous core statement in *Vogue* magazine in 1989: "A rat is a pig is a dog is a boy."

Randy Stiver, "Did God Give Animals Rights?" *Vertical Thought*, July–September 2007. Reproduced by permission. www.verticalthought.org/issues/vt16/animals.htm.

That statement summarizes the animal rights movement. It says that a human boy is morally the same as any other animal. But is that true? Who legitimately decides the moral value of a person or an animal—Peter Singer, Ingrid Newkirk, Tom Regan, Gary Francione or who?

God gave man dominion over all the animals.

Actually, the greatest ethicist and moralist in the history of ethics and morals decides—the Creator God, of course. But you knew that. God establishes value for all parts of His creation, and He did so from the beginning.

The first chapter in the entire Bible records the creation of all plants, bugs, fish, reptiles, mammals and mankind. "Then God said, 'Let Us make man in Our image, according to Our likeness; let them have dominion over the fish of the sea, over the birds of the air, and over the cattle, over all the earth and over every creeping thing that creeps on the earth.'"

Seven Keys to Understanding

There are seven critical keys to understanding the man/animal controversy.

1. God made man in His image. None of the animals in the creation were made in the image of God—only human beings. Bodily we are described as looking like God. Intellectually we reflect (albeit poorly) the divine mind. Of all God's creatures, only people have God-consciousness: "He has put [a sense of] eternity in their hearts."

2. God gave man dominion over all the animals. That mankind was the apex of God's creation is proven by the fact that God placed all the other creatures and the rest of creation under his rule and care.

Have people always taken good care of the animals? No, certainly not. Some have and do mistreat animals, including some in greed-driven, factory-farming methods employed in the mega-agriculture industry. God is not pleased about that. But the wrong actions of human beings do not elevate the moral standing of animals. People are still people in need of redemption, and animals are still animals.

Humanity Is Unique

3. God promises only human beings eternal life as His divine children in His Kingdom. Animals live here and now. Humanity is unique compared to all animals and even to the angels. Of Christ the Bible says: "For to which of the angels did He ever say: 'You are My Son, today I have begotten You'?" Amazingly, Christ calls us His brothers!

4. God gave human beings a mind vastly greater than that of any animal. Beavers build dams, but none ever developed the technologies to build a Hoover Dam or Aswan High Dam. Weaverbirds in Africa build beautiful, complex, community nests, but none has ever constructed the simplest apartment building.

This is the logical fallacy of the animal rights movement—it tries to make animals into pseudohumans.

Unlike the animals, man has a mastery of the creation. And no wonder, because God gave him a spirit essence in his mind that makes it possible. "For what man knows the things of a man except [by] the spirit of the man which is in him?"

Animals do not have the spirit in man that gives us such dynamic minds with God consciousness and profound self-awareness.

5. God made animals for the provision and enrichment of human beings. People were created to be children in the spirit family God is forming. Everything in the creation on earth, including the animals, He made for our provision, such as clothing and food; for our enrichment, through enjoyment of

their beauty and variety; and for helping us develop the qualities of divine character. Animals are powerful teaching tools in the hands of God.

6. The Bible doesn't talk about "animal rights." But God did give human beings responsibilities concerning animals. He commands and expects people to take care of animals as good stewards of His creation. "The godly are concerned for the welfare of their animals," but the wicked are cruel.

The six syllables of *anthropomorphizing* mean ascribing human attributes or characteristics to nonhuman animals, plants or things. This is the logical fallacy of the animal rights movement—it tries to make animals into pseudohumans. Cartoonists also personify animals, but their cartoons are funny because *almost* everyone knows that animals don't think and talk like human beings.

7. God alone defines true moral and ethical values—no matter how many philosophers conduct how many international conferences in how many universities. Because it rejects God's divine revelation as found in the Bible, human ethical philosophy draws wrong conclusions and has no moral authority. The animal rights movement has arbitrarily proclaimed artificial ethics. Like virtually all other human philosophy, it lacks vertical thinking skills.

So why do so many young men and women devote themselves to the animal rights movement? Perhaps it's because they are seeking meaning and purpose for their lives. Strangely, they're looking for God, but they just don't know it. Thus, they spend themselves in a vain cause based on wrong values. You, too, need meaning and purpose for your life. You need a cause, but *first* you need the truth.

Animals Are Not Moral Agents and So Cannot Have Rights

Tibor R. Machan

Tibor R. Machan is an author and professor of business ethics and Western civilization at Chapman University in Orange, California, as well as a research fellow at the Hoover Institution at Stanford University.

Since 1991 I have been arguing about animal rights and liberation. It came about because I wrote a paper, "Do Animals Have Rights?" after learning that a colleague, Tom Regan, had had a book prominently published by [the] University of California Press, *The Case for Animal Rights.* I had been writing on natural rights theory since I did my doctoral dissertation on the topic, and so I thought I needed to get straight about this animal rights issue.

My point was, in essence, that rights are just not the sort of things animals other than people could have. Could animals have guilt, be blamed, feel regret and remorse, or apologize or anything on that order? No, and why so, that was the gist of my thesis: They are not moral agents like us, not even the great apes.

If a non-human animal, however evolved, kills, maims or injures another animal of its own kind, we may lament this all we like, but to hold the perpetrator responsible just will not work. Animals are mostly instinctually driven to behave as they do, even if that may involve some slight measure of intelligence and self-awareness. What it does not involve is self-direction by means of free will, self-reflection and self-monitoring, all of what would enable them to initiate their conduct and to be morally responsible agents.

Tibor R. Machan, "Why Animal Rights Don't Exist," *Strike the Root*, March 14, 2004. Reproduced by permission. www.strike-the-root.com/4/machan/machan43.html.

Why do folks like Regan think animals have rights, nonetheless? Because they ascribe rights not on the basis of moral agency but because of a certain level of intelligence.

In nature there aren't very sharp divisions—a child doesn't become an adult at some precise point in time, a fetus doesn't become a child at some moment. Especially when it comes to biological entities, we leave off the precision of geometry and algebra. Instead there are areas of more or less grayness, as it were. And that's true about intelligence, too.

Yet this is no justification at all for abandoning the task of sensibly classifying things. And all in all it is human beings who have moral capacities, nothing else we know of, not even animals with some measure of intelligence—which, at any rate, tend to exhibit this intelligence mostly under prodding from human beings who capture them and start manipulating them to extend their smarts.

Yes, matters are more complicated than it was once thought, say by Rene Descartes, the great French philosopher who believed non-human animals were machines!

While there are some people who . . .—say when they're asleep or in a coma—lack moral agency, in general people possess that capacity, whereas non-people don't.

Putting Humans First

Recently I penned a book about this topic, *Putting Humans First*, expanding my earlier paper and developing the idea further to show that environmental ethics, too, is misguided by not recognizing that human beings are at the highest rung of nature and that conduct and public policy need to be forged with that in mind. No, this doesn't mean anything goes—torturing cats is still vicious, disregarding the pain of laboratory or household animals, or cattle or chicken, is wrong. But it doesn't follow that human goals and purposes do not justify our using animals.

Some have begun to take notice of my thesis since very few have gone on record about this—in part perhaps because PETA [People for the Ethical Treatment of Animals] and other animal activists are not a friendly bunch and most would just as soon stay out of their way. The most telling point against me goes as follows: "But there are people like very young kids, those in a coma, those with minimal mental powers, who also cannot be blamed, held responsible, etc., yet they have rights. Doesn't that show that other than human beings can have rights?"

This response doesn't recognize that classifications and ascriptions of capacities rely on the good sense of making certain generalizations. One way to show this is to recall that broken chairs, while they aren't any good to sit on, are still chairs, not monkeys or palm trees. Classifications are not something rigid but something reasonable. While there are some people who either for a little or longer while—say when they're asleep or in a coma—lack moral agency, in general people possess that capacity, whereas non-people don't. So it makes sense to understand them having rights so their capacity is respected and may be protected. This just doesn't work for other animals.

One last point. Some fault my approach for not proving with logical certainty that animals have no rights. But that is a mistaken demand—to prove a negative, like asking the defense to prove the innocence of the accused. It's animal rights proponents who haven't made the case for rights of animals, and I merely did some leg work to point that out.

Giving Animals Rights Is Antihuman

Wesley J. Smith

Wesley J. Smith is a senior fellow at the Discovery Institute and a special consultant to the Center for Bioethics and Culture.

If you are reading these words, you are a human being. That used to matter morally. Indeed, it was once deemed a self-evident truth that being a *Homo sapiens* [human] created intrinsic moral value based simply and merely on being human—a principle sometimes called "human exceptionalism."

No more. Human exceptionalism is under unprecedented assault across a broad array of societal and intellectual fronts. Bioethics . . . is a primary example. The predominating view among mainstream bioethicists is that human life per se does not matter morally. Rather, to be considered a full member of the moral community, one must achieve the status of being a "person" by possessing sufficient cognitive attributes such as being self-aware over time or being able to value one's life.

This approach creates a potentially disposable caste consisting of hundreds of millions of humans: all unborn life—early embryos may not have a brain, and fetuses are generally considered unconscious; infants—they have not yet developed sufficient capacities; and people like the late Terri Schiavo—who have lost requisite capacities through illness or injury. The point of personhood theory is insidious: It grants permission to kill human non-persons or use them as mere natural resources ripe for the harvest.

Bioethics is by no means the only existent threat to human exceptionalism and to its corollary, the sanctity/equality-of-human-life ethic. . . .

Wesley J. Smith, "Four Legs Good, Two Legs Bad: The Anti-human Values of 'Animal Rights,'" *Human Life Review*, Winter 2007, pp. 7–14. Copyright © Human Life Foundation, Incorporated 2007. Reproduced by permission. www.humanlifereview.com/2007_winter/win_2007Wesley_Smith1.pdf.

[Another] dangerous threat to the equality/sanctity-of-human-life ethic . . . comes from the animal-rights/liberation movement. Indeed, animal liberation is particularly subversive to our perceived status as a unique and special species because it advocates the creation of an explicit human/animal moral equality. Moreover, of the threats to human exceptionalism I have mentioned (and there are others), only animal-rights activists engage in significant violence and lawlessness to coerce society into accepting their values. Thus, not only is animal-rights/liberation a unique danger to human exceptionalism (particularly among the young), but it also presents a potent threat to the rule of law.

Beneath [PETA's] relatively benign facade lurks an ideologically absolutist movement that explicitly espouses equal moral worth between humans and animals.

Defenders of the sanctity/equality-of-human-life ethic need to combat animal rights. . . . To understand why, we need to look past the public image of animal-rights/liberation groups, such as the People for the Ethical Treatment of Animals (PETA), as committed animal lovers who engage in wacky advocacy tactics such as posing nude to protest fur. For beneath this relatively benign facade lurks an ideologically absolutist movement that explicitly espouses equal moral worth between humans and animals.

What's wrong with wanting to protect animals? Absolutely nothing. Indeed, advocating for animal welfare can be a noble cause. But this isn't the ultimate agenda of animal rights/liberation. Thus, to understand the profound threat the movement poses to human exceptionalism, it must be distinguished from the animal-welfare movement.

The first distinguishing factor between animal rights and animal welfare is that, unlike the former ideology, the latter approach accepts human exceptionalism. As a consequence, animal welfarists argue that while human beings may have a right to use animals for our betterment and enjoyment, we also have a fundamental duty to do so in a proper and humane manner. Welfarists also believe we have a human duty to prevent unnecessary animal suffering. Thus, they engage in activities such as neutering feral cats and campaigning on behalf of more humane methods of slaughtering food animals.

A Radical Departure

In contrast, animal rights/liberation—while often engaging in welfare type actions—is actually a radical departure from animal welfare. Whereas welfarists urge steady improvement of our treatment of animals and take actions to reduce animal suffering, the goal of the liberationists is to completely *end* every human use of animals. Thus, Gary L. Francione, director of the Rutgers University Animal Rights Law Center, seeks the eradication "of the property status of animals." In his view there should ultimately be no domesticated animals. Similarly, PETA asserts that "animals are not ours to use—for food, clothing, entertainment, experimentation, or any other reason."

To truly understand the subversive nature of the animal-rights philosophy, we have to look deeply into the movement's ultimate beliefs. For example, is the life of a monkey as precious as that of a human being? Animal rights believers say yes. Is butchering a cow morally equivalent to lynching a black man during the Jim Crow era? PETA's "Animal Liberation Project" explicitly stated that it is. Is artificially inseminating turkeys the moral equivalent of rape? Yes, according to Gary Francione, who criticized Peter Singer (and a colleague) for participating in a turkey-insemination demonstration. "I suggest that there is no non-speciesist way to justify what Singer and Mason claim to have done," Francione raged, "without also justifying the rape of a woman, or the molestation of a child, in order to see what those acts of violence 'really involved.'" Many animal-rights activists and academics assert that animals should be considered "persons" with legal rights including full standing in the courts. Legislation will soon be introduced in Spain to grant full personhood rights to great apes.

Animal liberationists fervently *reject any hierarchy of moral worth between humans and animals.*

We cannot fully comprehend why animal liberationists believe these things—and why the most radical among them act violently against those they consider animal abusers—without understanding that liberationists *fervently* reject any hierarchy of moral worth between humans and animals. And this raises an important question: If being human does not convey moral worth to the liberationist, what does?

Two Approaches to Animal Rights

Space doesn't permit a complete exposition of all aspects and every nuance of animal-rights ideology. For our purposes, it is sufficient to explore the two primary ideological approaches: one that focuses on sentience as the source of moral value, and another that focuses on what has been called "painience," that is, the ability to feel pain.

Rutgers's Gary Francione is the best-known animal-liberation theorist advocating sentience as the primary measurement of moral value. "I argue that all sentient beings should have one right: the right not to be treated as our property—the right not to be valued exclusively as means to human ends," Francione stated in an interview. . . . In this view, since animals are not unconscious, they have a "right" not to be used instrumentally. Hence, each and every human use of animals—no matter how seemingly benign—is as wrong as if the same use were made of a non-consenting human being.

Thus, to the true liberationist, cattle ranching is as odious as slavery because cows and humans are both sentient beings.

Painience

The second primary approach to crafting moral equality between humans and animals takes a slightly different trail to arrive at the same anti-human destination. In this view, if a being is capable of feeling pain, that attribute alone creates "equality of the species." Richard Ryder, a former professor at Tulane University, has written that the ability to feel pain—a capacity he calls "painience"—is what confers moral worth. Since animals can feel pain, he writes, the goal should be to "gradually bring non-humans into the same moral and legal circle as ourselves," toward the end that we "will not be able to exploit them as our slaves."

PETA adopts the same concept in a slightly broader fashion. The issue for PETA is not just pain per se, but existential as well as physical suffering. Since PETA asserts that any use of animals by humans causes suffering, the group opposes sheep raising and wool shearing, eating dairy products, zoos, medical research using animals—even seeing-eye dogs. Or as Ingrid Newkirk, the head of PETA, once infamously stated, "There is no rational basis for saying that a human being has special rights. A rat is a pig is a dog is a boy." Illustrating the profound harm to human welfare that would result from society's acceptance of animal-rights/liberation ideology, when Newkirk was asked if she would sacrifice five thousand rats or chimpanzees if it would result in a cure for AIDS, she retorted, "Would you be opposed to experiments on your daughter if you knew it would save fifty million people?"

The Utilitarian View

At this point, we need to consider the beliefs of Peter Singer, who is often called the godfather of animal rights because his 1975 book *Animal Liberation* is widely seen as having jump-started the modern movement. But unlike the true animal liberationist, Singer is not explicitly opposed to all animal research, or even, necessarily, to the eating of meat. . . . Instead, Singer is an "interest utilitarian," that is, he believes that actions are not right or wrong per se, but must be judged upon their anticipated or actual consequences. Under this view, those actions which best serve the interests of most (not necessarily human) beings are those that should be pursued.

Utilitarianism isn't new, of course. But Singer became notable by asserting in *Animal Liberation* that the interests of animals should be given "equal consideration" to the interests of people in making utilitarian analyses. To do otherwise, he declared, is "speciesism"—that is, discrimination against animals—a wrong as odious in his view as racism and sexism. Thus, when Singer was told recently that experiments on 100 monkeys benefited 40,000 people, he decreed that the experiment was "justifiable." But he would almost surely have said the same thing if the experiment had been with cognitively disabled human beings, since the interests of the many were served by using those with lesser capacities. Indeed Singer once suggested that cognitively disabled people, rather than chimps, should have been used in hepatitis-vaccine experiments—because the human beings have lower capacities than normal chimpanzees.

The great philosophical question of the 21st century is whether we will knock ourselves off of the pedestal of moral distinctiveness.

It is tempting to dismiss such assertions and beliefs as being so far into fringe territory that they are not worthy of serious concern. I believe the contrary is true. For many years the argument over animal rights has been generally one-sided: Supporters are vocal and energized, while those who oppose according animals "rights" are generally subdued. As a consequence, animal-rights values are seeping into public consciousness. For example, a 1995 Associated Press poll found that 67 percent of respondents agreed with the statement "an animal's right to live free of suffering is just as important as a person's right to live free of suffering." . . .

The animal-rights/liberation threat goes far beyond the philosophical. Because animal rights/liberationists believe that slaughtering animals for food is akin to murder, and that medical research using them is morally equivalent to [Nazi doctor Joseph] Mengele's experiments in the [Nazi-run] death camps [during World War II], violence in the name of saving animals is a growing threat. Indeed, according to John E. Lewis, deputy assistant director of the FBI's Counterterrorism Division, animal-rights terrorism has become one of the FBI's most urgent concerns: "One of today's most serious domestic terrorism threats comes from special interest extremist movements such as the Animal Liberation Front (ALF), the Earth Liberation Front (ELF), and Stop Huntingdon Animal Cruelty (SHAC) campaign. Adherents to these movements aim to resolve specific issues by using criminal 'direct action' against individuals or companies believed to be abusing or exploiting animals or the environment." . . .

Reducing Evil to the Banal

Most people, particularly those in the pro-life movement, take human exceptionalism for granted. They can no longer afford to do so. The great philosophical question of the 21st century is whether we will knock ourselves off of the pedestal of moral distinctiveness. The stakes of this debate over human exceptionalism, which includes but is not limited to the animal-rights issue, could not be more important. After all, it is our exalted moral status that both bestows special rights upon us and imposes unique and solemn moral responsibilities—including the human duty not to abuse animals.

Unfortunately, the liberationists are oblivious to this point. By denying our unique status as human beings they dilute the very concept of evil and reduce it to the banal. Slavery is evil: Raising sheep is not even wrong. The Rwandan and Cambodian genocides were evil: Humanely slaughtering millions of animals to provide the multitudes with nourishing food is not even wrong. Rape is evil: Inseminating mares and milk cows is not even wrong. Mengele's human experiments were pure evil: Testing new drugs or surgical procedures on animals to save children's lives is not even wrong.

Even more fundamentally, the way we act toward one another and the world is based substantially on the nature of the beings we perceive ourselves to be. In this sense, the entire planet will rue the day that liberationists succeed in convincing society that there is no justification for the reigning hierarchy of moral worth. After all, if we ever came to consider ourselves as just another animal in the forest, that would be precisely how we would act.

Animals Need Better Care, Not Equal Rights

Jon Katz

Jon Katz is a former television producer, a media critic, a journalist, and author of several books.

In Defense of Animals [IDA], a California-based animal rights organization, sent me [in February 2004] some materials about its *Guardian Campaign*. A polite letter complimented me on my most recent book, then requested that I use the term "guardian" rather than "owner" in future writings about dogs.

The benefits of relating to animals as guardians rather than as owners would be "far reaching," wrote IDA president Dr. Elliot Katz (who's no relation). Changing how we speak would help change how we act. In a world where dogs are protected rather than *owned*, Katz argued, it would be easier to crack down on animal abuse, end the puppy-mill trade, and stop the killing of animals at shelters.

Turning Animals into Humans

As a dog lover, owner of a rescue dog, and member of two rescue groups, I'm not convinced there will be concrete benefits from this metaphoric, even Orwellian revolution [George Orwell's philosophy was that certain conditions were detrimental to a free society]. How exactly will these semantic changes improve the lot of animals? Why can't we shut down puppy mills, end some cruel animal research, save the lives of dogs and cats in shelters, prosecute animal abuse, and *still* call ourselves "owners"?

IDA's letter proudly pointed out that San Francisco; West Hollywood; Berkeley, Calif.; Boulder, Colo.; Amherst, Mass.,

Jon Katz, "Guarding the Guard Dogs? Are You a Dog 'Owner'—or a Dog 'Guardian'?" *Slate*, March 5, 2004. Copyright © 2004 Washingtonpost/Newsweek Interactive. All rights reserved. www.slate.com/id/2096577/.

and the state of Rhode Island have already enacted ordinances changing owners into guardians. (Some of those jurisdictions have also embraced the animal-rights movement's other language crusade, changing "pets" into "companion animals.") Although IDA cited these cities and state as evidence that the notion of "guardian" is spreading, to me it suggests the opposite: Its successes are confined to left-wing pockets. I'll be impressed when Kansas City takes up the idea.

Social movements are only as effective as their ability to win popular support. I'm currently living in rural upstate New York, and I showed the IDA packet to Sandra, a sheep farmer who lives down the road with her female partner. She was shocked. "I love my Rottweiler," Sandra told me. "But I'd love to marry my partner and I can't. I have to say I'm a bit uncomfortable with dogs having more rights than I do. Me first." Sandra had just filed legal papers to have her partner declared her legal guardian in the event of serious illness. She said she was not about to do the same for her dog.

Easing animal suffering is inarguably worthwhile; turning animals into a kind of human is another matter.

I reminded Sandra that animal rights don't really come at the expense of human rights—there's no reason both species can't have some protection. But her reservations are important. Easing animal suffering is inarguably worthwhile; turning animals into a kind of human is another matter.

And such a transformation seems the goal of some animal activists. My IDA packet contained a testimonial from a Michael Mountain of the Best Friends Animal Sanctuary. "People of other genders, races and even age groups were once treated as property in this country," Mountain wrote. "Now, it is time for 'people' of other species to be accorded the same simple dignity of being recognized, not as someone else's property but as beings in their own right." Mountain couldn't have made the point more dramatically—or offensively. I don't care to jump in with a moral value system that equates my beloved border collies with human slaves. Nothing about this comparison helps animals. It distorts their true natures and diminishes ours.

The guardian campaign is a vivid example of the growing tendency to blur the boundaries between us and our pets. Many Americans have already stopped seeing their dogs and cats as animals. They're family members, emotional support systems, metaphors for issues from our own pasts, aids for healing and growth, children with fur.

Another Kind of Abuse

Seeing them the way we see ourselves—as having human thoughts and needs, human rights—is another kind of abuse and exploitation. It is cruel to crate a child, but it's often helpful and soothing to crate a dog. No human would want to spend five minutes in a kennel, yet good kennels, much maligned by deeply attached pet owners, are often the safest and best places to leave dogs when we leave home.

Seeing dogs as piteous, deprived, abused, and needy can lead us to treat them unwisely. Vets cite overfeeding and the resultant epidemic obesity as a major killer of dogs and cats in America. Yet I can't count how many times I've heard somebody say, "I feed him because I just can't bear to starve him." Or "I just can't resist when he begs for food. He's so cute." Any vet or animal nutritionist would tell these people that they're doing as much harm to their cute little beggars by overfeeding them as they would by kicking them.

People who see their dogs as humanlike often struggle to train them properly, especially if they believe they were abused or mistreated. Owners sometimes think their dogs have already suffered so much that they couldn't possibly inflict any more criticism. Yet it's that very firm, effective training that would make those dogs happier and more secure. And what about the growing number of owners who find neutering cruel or unbearable, because they would find it so? Refusing to neuter may put their own pet or someone else's in danger—causing aggression, running away, and unwanted litters. Or the pet owners who make their dogs hyper by believing they need to "play" continuously, like overprogrammed boomer children? They drag them to unruly play groups, toss Frisbees and balls night and day, haul them to an endless round of organized activities—but fail to teach them how to be calm.

Dogs are not "people" of another species. They are another species.

The humanlike view of dogs affects the decision about when to euthanize a sick or elderly pet. I recently attended two veterinary conventions where scores of vets told me their biggest recent problem is people who see their pets as so human that they simply cannot end their lives or suffering, no matter the cost or the pain.

There is no evidence that dogs have the kind of complex emotional lives and value systems that we do. It's one reason why we love them so much, in fact. They are neither "good" nor "bad." They don't hold grudges, act in petty ways, or seek revenge. They read our moods, but not our minds. If they did, we'd start loving them as we love other humans—which could mean a lot less than we love them now.

Dogs are not "people" of another species. They *are* another species. To train and care for them properly, to show them how to live in our complex world, requires first and foremost that we understand that. I owe my dogs much—more than I can say—but they are not my "companions"—as if we voluntarily chose to hang out together but none of us has authority over the others. I bought and/or acquired them. I own them. I am profoundly responsible for their care and well being.

Guardianship, a word always applied to human beings, implies *equality*—the highest and perhaps most noble of all goals in this democratic nation. Ownership implies *responsibility.* Americans who own dogs need to be more responsible for them, literally and emotionally—not more equal to them.

The drama of the modern dog is that he is segregated from society—from work, children, public places—and then blamed for not knowing how to live in our world. The things he wants to do—have sex, roll in gross stuff, roam freely, squabble with other dogs, chew shoes, pee on every other tree—are either illegal or frowned upon. His challenge isn't to become a free and equal person in the best traditions of our society but to learn how to live in the alien world of people.

Guardianship suggests dogs have a right to live their own lives as they wish. This is impossible in our dog-unfriendly world. Ownership implies a human duty to help the dog adjust to this difficult, inhospitable place.

"Dog owner" is a proud title. It suits me fine.

CHAPTER 2

Does the Food Industry Mistreat Animals?

Chapter Preface

One of the issues that most concerns animal rights activists is the treatment of farm animals. Contrary to the ideal of bucolic farm life where animals happily graze on open pastures under sunny skies, most farms today are more like factories, where animals are housed in very confined conditions and generally treated as commodities, in order to maximize production of meat, eggs, and milk. Presently, most of these animals receive almost no legal protection from inhumane farming and slaughter practices. As a Web site of the Humane Society of the United States explains:

> In the United States, 10 billion land animals are raised and killed annually by the meat, egg, and dairy industries. Despite the incredible number of individuals and the routine suffering too many endure, these farm animals do not receive protection under the federal Animal Welfare Act. Moreover, 95 percent of the animals slaughtered each year do not receive protection under the federal Humane Methods of Slaughter Act. And, while each state has its own animal cruelty code, most states exempt common farming practices, no matter how abusive. As a result, across the country, billions of farm animals are denied virtually any protection from the cruelties and inhumane conditions on today's factory farms.

At the federal level, the only comprehensive law that governs treatment of animals is the Animal Welfare Act (AWA), which was signed in 1966. This law, however, only regulates the treatment of animals in research, exhibition, transport, commerce, and by dealers. Basically, this includes certain animals (other than birds, reptiles, rats, and mice) in medical laboratories, dealers who sell animals to laboratories, animal exhibitors, carriers and intermediate handlers, dog and cat breeders, puppy mills, zoos, circuses, roadside menageries, and transporters of animals. The U.S. Department of Agriculture

(USDA), which is responsible for enforcement, interprets the act to completely exclude farm animals, such as cows, pigs, and horses, which are used or slaughtered for food or fiber. The AWA only applies to farm animals when they are used in biomedical research, testing, teaching, or exhibition.

Two other federal laws provide minimal rules for certain specific farm animal practices. The Humane Methods of Slaughter Act, also enforced by the USDA, requires that livestock—such as cows, horses, mules, sheep, and pigs—be slaughtered humanely. Specifically, the act provides that meatpacking plants slaughter animals either by using Jewish kosher methods; by rendering them insensible to pain by a single blow or gunshot; or by an electrical, chemical, or other rapid and effective method. Also, under the "Twenty-Eight Hour Law," farm animals must not be confined in trucks or other vehicles for more than twenty-eight consecutive hours without unloading the animals for food and water.

Several bills are pending in Congress that could give farm animals a bit more protection, but they are far from comprehensive and their passage is uncertain. One of these is the Farm Animal Stewardship Purchasing Act (H.R. 1726), which would require producers supplying meat, dairy products, or eggs to the military, federal prisons, school lunches, and other federal programs to comply with basic animal welfare requirements. Another proposal is the Downed Animal and Food Safety Protection Act (S. 394 and H.R. 661), which would prohibit the use of sick or injured animals to make human food and require that these "downed" animals be immediately and humanely euthanized. Other pending bills seek to curb the overuse of antibiotics in factory farms and require the proper labeling of cloned animals.

At the state and local level, there are several efforts underway to prevent cruelty and improve the lives of farm animals. In 2006, for example, voters in Arizona overwhelmingly passed a historic initiative to improve the lives of farm animals—the

Humane Treatment of Farm Animals Act. This law, supported by 62 percent of voters, prohibits two factory farming practices that are widely viewed as cruel and abusive: the confinement of calves in veal crates and the confinement of pregnant pigs in gestation crates. Crates are used by meat producers to maximize profitability and efficiency in veal and pork production, but they force animals to live out their entire lives without enough room to turn around, lie down, or even extend their limbs. Florida passed similar legislation in 2002 banning pig gestation crates, and a measure is also gathering support in California. An initiative called the California Prevention of Farm Cruelty Act, if it reaches the 2008 ballot and is passed by voters, would outlaw the crating of calves and pigs, as well as the confinement of egg-laying chickens in tiny "battery cages," as they're known in the industry, with numerous other birds where they cannot even spread their wings. Several other states and localities have also passed legislation against chicken battery cages.

Many of these animal protection initiatives were proposed and supported by animal rights and animal welfare groups, and opposed by meat, dairy, and egg producers. Farm companies claim their practices are not cruel and are necessary to keep food prices low, but increasingly animal advocates are convincing the public that farm animals deserve better treatment. The viewpoints in this chapter illustrate the many different facets of this important issue.

Factory Farming Ignores the Suffering of Animals

Peter Singer, Interviewed by Oliver Broudy

Peter Singer is the DeCamp Professor of Bioethics at Princeton University who is often cited by animal rights groups. Oliver Broudy is a writer and a former editor of the Paris Review. *whose work has appeared in the* New York Times *and* Mother Jones.

Peter Singer is a professional ethicist. Best known for his 1975 book *Animal Liberation*—a canonical text of the animal rights movement and the inspiration for untold thousands to take up vegetarianism—Singer, in the last quarter-plus century, has published a string of books on everything from test tube babies to the ethics of [President] George W. Bush. Considered fearless by some, and dangerous by others, virtually all agree that he is among the most influential philosophers alive today. . . .

*Oliver Broudy: One of the things that distinguishes your new book [*The Way We Eat: Why Our Food Choices Matter*] is all the field research that went into it. What most shocked you, over the course of doing this research?*

Peter Singer: Probably this video I saw of this kosher slaughterhouse, *AgriProcessors*. I guess I had this idea that kosher slaughter is more strictly controlled than normal slaughter, and when you see that video and you see these cattle staggering around with their throats cut, and blood pouring out—by no stretch of the imagination is this just a reflex movement. It goes on and on. And this happens repeatedly, with many different animals.

Oliver Broudy, "The Practical Ethicist: 'The Way We Eat' Author Peter Singer Explains the Advantage of Wingless Chickens, How Humans Discriminate Against Animals, and the Downside of Buying Locally Grown Food," *Salon*, May 8, 2006. This article first appeared in Salon.com, at www.salon.com. An online version remains in the *Salon* archives. Reprinted with permission.

How are kosher animals supposed to be slaughtered?

They are supposed to be slaughtered with a single blow of a sharp knife across the throat. There's a virtually instant loss of consciousness, because the brain loses blood so quickly. That's the idea, anyway. But when you see this video, it's so far from that, I really did find it quite shocking.

You mention in your book that cows today produce three times as much milk as they did 50 years ago. That's a great advance, isn't it?

It is an advance, but you have to consider how this has been achieved. Fifty years ago, cows were basically fed on grass. They walked around and selected their food themselves, food that we can't eat, chewing it up and producing milk that we *can* eat. Now cows are confined indoors, and a lot of their food supply is grown specifically for them, on land that we could have used to grow food for ourselves. So it's actually less efficient, in that we could have gotten more food from the land if we didn't pass it through the cow.

[Even in an organic farm] there were no hens outside at all. The hens were all in these huge sheds, about 20,000 hens in a single shed, and they were pretty crowded.

Most of us have an idealized notion of what an organic farm is like. You visited an organic chicken farm in New Hampshire. Did it meet your expectations?

I have to say that it didn't. I guess I was expecting some access to pasture for the hens. When I got to this place, although it was in a beautiful green valley in New Hampshire, and it was a fine, sunny fall day, there were no hens outside at all. The hens were all in these huge sheds, about 20,000 hens in a single shed, and they were pretty crowded. The floor of the shed was basically a sea of brown hens, and when we asked about access to outdoors, we were shown a small dirt run which at the best of times I don't think the hens would be very interested in. In any case the doors were closed, and when we asked why, we were told that the producer was worried about bird flu. So, yes, it was not really what I expected. It was still a kind of a factory farm production—although undoubtedly it was much better than a caged operation.

How much space are birds allotted in caged operations?

In the U.S., birds have as little as 48 square inches, a six-by eight-inch space. The United Egg Producers' standards are gradually increasing over the next five years. We'll get up to 67 square inches. But that's still not the industry average, and even 67 square inches is just [the size of] a sheet of standard letter paper. In a cage, the birds are unable to stretch their wings. The wingspan of the bird is about 31 inches, so even if you lined one bird up on the diagonal, she wouldn't be able to spread her wings. And there's not just one bird in these cages, there are four or five. The weaker birds are unable to escape from the more aggressive birds. They end up rubbing against the wire and getting pecked, so they lose a lot of feathers, and they can't lay their eggs in the nesting box.

Requiring a hen to lay in an open space [is like] asking a human to shit in public. They don't like it.

One good thing about this organic farm in New Hampshire is that there was this row of nesting boxes. It's been shown that hens have a strong instinct to lay in this kind of sheltered area. Conrad Lawrence, the science fiction writer and author of *The Council to Save the Planet*, once compared requiring a hen to lay in an open space to asking a human to shit in public. They don't like it.

What if it were possible to genetically engineer a brainless bird, grown strictly for its meat? Do you feel that this would be ethically acceptable?

It would be an ethical improvement on the present system, because it would eliminate the suffering that these birds are feeling. That's the huge plus to me.

What if you could engineer a chicken with no wings, so less space would be required?

I guess that's an improvement too, assuming it doesn't have any residual instincts, like phantom pain. If you could eliminate various other chicken instincts, like its preference for laying eggs in a nest, that would be an improvement too.

It seems to come down to a trade-off between whether the bird has wing space or whether you can fit more birds in your shed, and therefore have to pay less heating costs. How does one go about weighing these alternatives? How does the ethicist put a price on the impulse of a chicken to spread its wings?

We ought to be prepared to pay more for eggs so that the chicken can enjoy its life, and not be frustrated and deprived and miserable.

We recognize the chicken as another conscious being. It's different from us, but it has a life, and if something is really important for that chicken, if it would work hard to try to get it, and if we can give it without sacrificing something that's really important to us, then we should. If it's a big burden on us, that's surely different, but if it's a question of paying a few more cents for eggs, when we pay just as much if not more for a brand label we like, then we ought to be prepared to pay more for eggs so that the chicken can enjoy its life, and not be frustrated and deprived and miserable.

What constitutes a big burden? Doubtless the chicken farmer would say that building a larger shed or paying a bigger heating bill is a big burden.

It's only a burden to him if it harms his business, and it only harms his business if he can't sell the eggs he produces because other producers who don't follow those standards are selling eggs more cheaply. So, there's two ways around that: Either you have ethically motivated consumers who are prepared to pay a somewhat higher price for humanely certified eggs, or you cut out the unfair competition with regulations. Prohibiting cages, for example. And that's been done already, in Switzerland. And the entire European Union is already saying you can't keep hens as confined as American hens; it's on track to require nesting boxes, and areas to scratch, by 2012. So you can do it, and it doesn't mean that people can no longer afford to eat eggs.

In your book you discuss this in terms of the right of the chicken to express its natural behavior.

I tend not to put it in terms of rights, because philosophically I have doubts about the foundations of rights. But yes, I think these animals have natural behaviors, and generally speaking, their natural behaviors are the ones they have adapted for. And if we prevent them from performing those natural behaviors, we are likely to be frustrating them and making them miserable. So, yes, I think we ought to try to let them perform those natural behaviors.

We have, over centuries of history, expanded the circle of beings whom we regard as morally significant.

Could you explain your position on "speciesism," and what this has to do with your call to "expand the circle"?

The argument, in essence, is that we have, over centuries of history, expanded the circle of beings whom we regard as morally significant. If you go back in time you'll find tribes that were essentially only concerned with their own tribal members. If you were a member of another tribe, you could be killed with impunity. When we got beyond that there were still boundaries to our moral sphere, but these were based on nationality, or race, or religious belief. Anyone outside those boundaries didn't count. Slavery is the best example here. If you were not a member of the European race, if you were African, specifically, you could be enslaved. So we got beyond that. We have expanded the circle beyond our own race and we reject as wrongful the idea that something like race or religion or gender can be a basis for claiming another being's interests count less than our own.

So the argument is that this is also an arbitrary stopping place; it's also a form of discrimination, which I call "speciesism," that has parallels with racism. I am not saying it's identical, but in both cases you have this group that has power over the outsiders, and develops an ideology that says, Those outside our circle don't matter, and therefore we can make use of them for our own convenience.

I don't think we can say that somehow we, as humans, are the sole repository of all moral value, and that all beings beyond our species don't matter.

That is what we have done, and still do, with other species. They're effectively *things*; they're property that we can own, buy and sell. We use them as is convenient and we keep them in ways that suit us best, producing products we want at the cheapest prices. So my argument is simply that this is wrong, this is not justifiable if we want to defend the idea of human equality against those who have a narrower definition. I don't think we can say that somehow we, as humans, are the sole repository of all moral value, and that all beings beyond our species don't matter. I think they do matter, and we need to expand our moral consideration to take that into account.

So you are saying that expanding the circle to include other species is really no different than expanding it to include other races?

Yes, I think it's a constant progression, a broadening of that circle.

But surely there's a significant difference between a Jew, for instance, and a chicken. These are different orders of beings.

Well, of course, there's no argument about that. The question is whether saying that you are not a member of my kind, and that therefore I don't have to give consideration to your interests, is something that was said by the Nazis and the slave traders, and is also something that we are saying to other species. The question is, what is the relevant difference here? There is no doubt that there is a huge difference between human and nonhuman animals. But what we are overlooking is the fact that nonhuman animals are conscious beings, that they can suffer. And we ignore that suffering, just as the Nazis ignored the suffering of the Jews, or the slave traders ignored the suffering of the Africans. I'm not saying that it's the same sort of suffering. I am not saying that factory farming is the same as the Holocaust or the slave trade, but it's clear that there is an immense amount of suffering in it, and just as we think that the Nazis were wrong to ignore the suffering of their victims, so we are wrong to ignore the sufferings of our victims.

But how do you know at what point to stop expanding the circle?

I think it gets gray when you get beyond mammals, and certainly it gets grayer still when you get beyond vertebrates. That's something we don't know enough about yet. We don't understand the way the nervous systems of invertebrates work. . . .

Chickens get some slaughterhouse remnants in their feed, . . . so that could be a route by which mad-cow disease gets . . . into the cattle.

I wanted to list a few factoids that jumped out at me while reading your book, and if you want to comment on them I'd love to hear your thoughts. First, each of the 36 million cattle produced in the United States has eaten 66 pounds of chicken litter?

The chicken industry produces a vast amount of litter that the chickens are living on, which of course gets filled with the chicken excrement, and is cleaned maybe once a year. And then the question is, what [do] you do with it? Well, it's been discovered that cattle will eat it. But the chickens get some slaughterhouse remnants in their feed, and some of that feed they may not eat, so the slaughterhouse remnants may also be in the chicken litter. So that could be a route by which mad-cow disease gets from these prohibited slaughterhouse products into the cattle, through this circuitous route.

A local chicken farm was getting rid of hens at the end of their laying period by throwing them by the bucketload down a wood chipper.

Second factoid: 284 gallons of oil go into fattening a 1,250-pound cow for slaughter?

That's a figure from David Pimentel, a Cornell [University] ecologist. The fossil fuel goes into the fertilizer used to fertilize these acres of grain, which are then harvested and processed and transported to the cattle for feed. We get back, at most, 10 percent of the food value of the grain that we put into the cattle. So we are just skimming this concentrated product off the top of a mountain of grain into which all this fossil fuel has gone.

So even if we all started driving Priuses we'd still have these cows to worry about.

Yes. In fact, there's a University of Chicago study that shows that if you switch from driving an American car to driving a Prius, you'll cut your carbon-dioxide emissions by one ton per year. But if you switch from a typical U.S. diet, about 28 percent of which comes from animal sources, to a vegan diet with the same number of calories, you'll cut your carbon-dioxide emissions by nearly 1.5 tons per year.

Third factoid: We have more people in prison in the United States than people whose primary occupation is working on a farm?

Isn't that amazing? Just as an example, when I wrote *Animal Liberation* 30 years ago or so, there were more than 600,000 independent pig farms in the U.S. Now there are only about 60,000. We're still producing just as many pigs, in fact more pigs, but there has been such concentration that we are now producing more pigs with a tenth as many pig farms. The same has happened in dairy and many other areas.

Avoid factory farm products. The worst of all the things . . . is intensive animal agriculture.

And finally, it turns out that a wood chipper is not the best way to dispose of 10,000 spent hens?

Yes, this also came to mind when you asked me what most shocked me. This was in San Diego County, in California. Neighbors noticed that a local chicken farm was getting rid of hens at the end of their laying period by throwing them by the bucketload down a wood chipper. They complained to the Animal Welfare Department, which investigated, and the chicken farmer told them that this was a recommendation that had been made by their vet, a vet who happens to sit on the Animal Welfare Committee of the American Veterinary Medical Association. The American Veterinary Medical Association, I should say, does not condone throwing hens down a wood chipper, but it is apparently done. We've also had examples of hens being taken off the conveyor belt and simply dumped into a bin, where by piling more hens on top, the hens on the bottom were suffocated. These old hens have no value, that's the problem, and so people have been killing them by whatever means is cheapest and most convenient.

So if you were stuck with 10,000 spent hens, what would you do with them?

I think you have a responsibility. Those hens have been producing eggs for you for a year or 18 months. You have a responsibility to make sure they are killed humanely. And you can do that. You can truck them to a place where there is stunning, or, better still, you can bring stunning equipment to the farm, and you can make sure that every hen is individually stunned with an electric shock and then killed by having its throat cut.

I thought you might suggest a retirement program.

That's an ideal that some people would like to see, but if you have to maintain and feed hens when they are no longer laying eggs, that will significantly increase the cost of the egg, and even the organic farms don't do that.

After reading this interview, some readers might be inspired to change their diets. If you could suggest one thing, what would it be?

Avoid factory farm products. The worst of all the things we talk about in the book is intensive animal agriculture. If you can be vegetarian or vegan that's ideal. If you can buy organic and vegan that's better still, and organic and fair trade and vegan, better still, but if that gets too difficult or too complicated, just ask yourself, Does this product come from intensive animal agriculture? If it does, avoid it, and then you will have achieved 80 percent of the good that you would have achieved if you followed every suggestion in the book.

The Animal Agriculture Industry Cares About the Welfare of Animals

Charles W. Stenholm

Charles W. Stenholm was a member of the U.S. House of Representatives from Texas from 1979 to 2005. He is now a lobbyist who represents various agricultural interests. The following viewpoint is taken from Stenholm's testimony before the House Committee on Agriculture's Subcommittee on Livestock, Dairy, and Poultry, on May 8, 2007.

If you eat or wear clothes, you are affected by agriculture. The industry remains an important part of the United States economy, and according to the U.S. Department of Agriculture (USDA), animal products account for the majority (51 percent) of the value of U.S. agricultural products, exceeding $100 billion per year. As a farmer and rancher, I believe in the significance of the agriculture industry and in the value animal agriculture producers put on the safety and welfare of their livestock. . . .

With over 130 years of racing history at Churchill Downs [site of the Kentucky Derby], it is clear that the owners, trainers, and riders of the Derby care about the welfare of their animals. I'm sure many of you went to zoos as a child or will bring your children and grandchildren to one this summer. In fact, more people attend zoos every year than all sporting events combined, and the caregivers at zoos nationwide care about the welfare of their animals. Many of you probably remember the first time you saw the circus and may attend when it comes here. The Ringling Brothers and Barnum & Bailey Center for Elephant Conservation has one of the most

Testimony of Congressman Charles W. Stenholm to the House Committee on Agriculture, Subcommittee on Livestock, Dairy, and Poultry, May 8, 2007. http://agricult ure.house.gov/testimony/110/h70508/Stenholm.DOC.

successful breeding programs for endangered Asian elephants outside of Southeast Asia. They care about the welfare of their animals. Just like these groups of animal owners, production agriculture has not been given the credit it is due by animal "rights" activists, and we, too, care about the welfare of our animals. There is one thing that everyone agrees on: all animals should be treated humanely from birth to death. . . .

Livestock Producers Care About Animals

Livestock producer associations . . . all care about the same thing: ensuring the health and well-being of their animals is their number one priority. The livestock industry has worked hard both from a legislative standpoint and through industry guidelines to improve animal welfare conditions. Animal agriculture constantly works to accept new technologies and science and apply them to the industry, investing millions of dollars every year to ensure the wellness of their livestock. Producers recognize the need to maintain animal welfare regulations for the safety and nutrition of their livestock, for the conservation of the environment, and for the profitability of their operations. But those regulations should be based on sound science from veterinary professionals that best understand animals, working together with legitimate animal use industries.

Many of the livestock groups have quality assurance programs in place. For example, the New Jersey Legislature and Department of Agriculture commissioned Rutgers [University] in 2003 to perform a study on veal calf production, and experts at the land grant university concluded that the Veal Quality Assurance program and the principles behind it were scientifically sound. The poultry industry also continues to work on a united front to maintain a high level of oversight on animal welfare issues that ensures all employees practice the industry guidelines that were adopted. The animal agriculture industry continues to strive to improve animal health and welfare through scientific research, educational outreach, advocacy, legislation, and regulations.

Activist groups . . . have used falsehoods and scare tactics to push their hidden agendas of fundraising and systematically abolishing all use of animals.

While the livestock industry has a long history of supporting animal welfare, many activist groups such as PETA [People for the Ethical Treatment of Animals], the Humane Society of the United States (HSUS), and Farm Sanctuary have used falsehoods and scare tactics to push their hidden agendas of fundraising and systematically abolishing all use of animals, including production agriculture, zoos, circuses, and sporting events. These groups campaign for animal "rights," which is not synonymous with animal welfare, using half-truths or complete deception. For example, according to the American Veterinary Medical Association (AVMA), Farm Sanctuary charged veal farmers in New Jersey of malnutrition practices because of the absence of fiber in their calves' diets. However, a coalition of dairy farmers, animal nutrition specialists, and dairy extension specialists at Rutgers University testified that it is typical to not give calves fiber because it is not healthy for a calf's developing digestive system.

These groups also fail to mention the millions of dollars in fundraising and assets that drive their misguided goals. HSUS has accumulated $113 million in assets; has a budget three times the size of PETA's; and according to the Activist-Cash website, has more than enough funding to finance animal shelters in all fifty states, yet only operates one animal sanctuary, Black Beauty Ranch in Texas, which is at full capacity. According to the *Wall Street Journal*, two offshoots of HSUS spent $3.4 million on Congressional elections and ballot initiatives, which is more than Exxon Mobil Corp. [spent.]

And there is an ongoing investigation by the Louisiana attorney general to determine if the $30 million in HSUS fundraising during the Hurricane Katrina crisis has been handled appropriately.

These activist groups use the platform of animal "rights" to advocate for regulations so strict that they will put animal agriculture out of business (which is their real goal). A video recently circulated to Members of Congress and a video produced by HSUS make numerous false claims against the livestock industry. For example, the videos suggest that horses are inhumanely transported on double-decker trailers. However, a law exists that has banned the use of double-decker trailers for transporting horses on their way to slaughter, and if a horse does arrive on one of these trailers, the processing facilities will not accept it. In addition, numerous truck drivers invested in new trailers that comply with the law, and animal agriculture stepped up once again to improve animal welfare conditions.

More Misleading Rhetoric

Another example of the misleading rhetoric by animal "rights" activists involves the process of "captive bolt" euthanasia. The previously mentioned videos claim that captive bolt is not humane. However, the 2000 report of the AVMA's Panel on Euthanasia specifically approves the use of captive bolt as a humane technique of euthanasia for horses. It is also an approved method of euthanasia for pork, cattle, and lamb. The captive bolt method meets specific humane requirements set forth by AVMA's Panel on Euthanasia, USDA and the HSUS Statement on Euthanasia because it results in instantaneous brain death, and it is generally agreed to be the most humane method of euthanasia for livestock.

Watching the end of life for any living creature is not a pleasant experience, even when performed in the most humane manner. However, these groups continue to use human emotion and sensationalism to prey on the public's sensitivity in order to reach their goal of abolishing animal agriculture.

Protect America's Farmers and Ranchers

Unfortunately, we all know mistakes happen and laws are broken. I will not try to convince you otherwise. But when these unfortunate incidents occur, appropriate actions should be taken. We should not get in the habit of creating arbitrary, uninformed, and emotionally based regulations on an industry whose livelihood depends on the health and well-being of its animals. We should not tie the hands of researchers and investors that continually seek improvements in animal welfare practices, and we should not tie the hands of producers who work night and day to ensure the quality of life of their livestock so they can provide this country and others with the most abundant, safest, and most affordable food supply in the world.

Professional experts ... continue to have their expertise questioned by animal "rights" activists who line their own pockets with donations secured by exploiting and distorting the issues. These groups throw sensationalistic and often staged photos in the faces of those who do not understand [the issues] and ask them to give money to save the animals. But what they do not do is use their millions of dollars in fundraising to build animal shelters, provide research for new technologies and procedures or provide truthful information to consumers about the animal agriculture industry. Emotions run high, and with continued antics by activist groups the ultimate outcome will be devastating. If animal "rights" activist groups continue to be successful like we have seen in recent months with the closing of U.S. horse processing facilities, abandonment of animals will increase, animal welfare will decline, honest and legal businesses will close, America's trade balance will worsen, jobs will disappear, family heritage and livelihood will be stolen, and the best interest in the welfare of animals will be lost.

Factory Farms Mistreat Animals and Endanger Human Health

Kelly Overton

Kelly Overton is executive director of People Protecting Animals and Their Habitats, a nonprofit organization that advocates for the humane treatment of all animals and for the conservation of environments vital to the survival of endangered or threatened species.

Do the animal rights nuts know something we don't?

As we observe the growing number of avian flu cases worldwide, bide time until the eventual large-scale outbreak of mad cow disease in the United States and hope what the world experienced in 2004 wasn't just a dress rehearsal for SARS [severe acute respiratory disease, which caused a near-pandemic in 2003], the time has come to reconsider humanity's treatment of nonhuman animals—if only for the repercussions to our own health.

In past decades we have removed animals from pastures, sunshine and fresh air to stack them on top of each other in petri-dish-like buildings. As wild animals lose more and more of their habitats, they are forced to live on the perimeters of cities and towns and in a proximity to humans that increasingly appears to be detrimental not only to their health but also to ours.

Our health is being put at risk by our demand for low food prices. In the past decade consumers have chosen low prices over quality in the products and services we purchase—

Kelly Overton, "When Animals Suffer, So Do We," *The Washington Post*, April 12, 2006. Reproduced by permission of the author. www.washingtonpost.com/wp-dyn/con tent/article/2006/04/11/AR2006041101511.html.

but animals aren't products that can be endlessly manipulated for lower food costs. As a society it is time to ask ourselves if we are willing to trade our health and the health of our land, air and water in return for cheap milk, eggs and meat.

Because factory farms are legally recognized as farms—not the industrial sites they are—they are exempt from many of our most important environmental laws. The communities surrounding most factory farms have become wastelands from the constant flow of toxic emissions and waste polluting the air, ground and water. Inside the farms, safety and human health also take a back seat to profit. Animals too sick or diseased to stand are dragged or bulldozed to slaughter and into our food supply. Mad cow disease was born of such recklessness and greed—a desire by corporations to minimize financial losses by using the remains of diseased animals to feed the animals that enter our food supply.

Animals raised on a diet high in antibiotics ensure human consumption of antibiotics, decreasing their effectiveness when we need them to fight infection. The presence of antibiotics in our food and water also encourages the emergence of drug-resistant illnesses. In fact, an increasing number of public health issues are linked to our mistreatment of nonhuman animals—including the growing human resistance to antibiotics and the many health consequences of global warming.

Animal-borne diseases may very well achieve what human activism has failed to do—guarantee nonhuman animals more humane lives.

Meanwhile, the change from a nation whose food was once supplied by thousands of small- to medium-size farms spread across the country to a nation now dependent on just a few factory farms in specific areas is inviting disaster. This new concentration of meat and food production in specific geographic corridors allows for one incident of accidental contamination, sabotage or terrorist activity to cripple our food supply.

Creutzfeldt-Jakob disease, or CJD, the human version of bovine spongiform encephalopathy (mad cow disease), can lie dormant for up to 40 years. Once discovered it is too late— the disease has proved fatal in every human case to date. The repercussions to human health from factory farming and habitat destruction may not be known for decades, or they may immediately fly into our daily lives via an avian flu pandemic.

Time for Change

It is ironic that animal-borne diseases may very well achieve what human activism has failed to do—guarantee nonhuman animals more humane lives by making animal welfare synonymous with human welfare. Regardless of how our society arrives at the conclusion, it is time to end one of the most inhumane and shameful chapters in our nation's history.

We humans remain only one species in what has always been a global ecosystem—an interlinked web of life where the health of one species depends on the health of others. Whether through reckless factory farming, the pollution of waters and the poisoning of the species within them, or the continued rampant destruction of forests and nonhuman habitat, our blatant mistreatment of other species for the benefit of our own is not inviting disaster, it's guaranteeing it. It is time to end the treatment of God's living creatures as products and to begin treating all life forms with respect and reverence before the health repercussions to the human species are irreparable.

Modern Animal Agriculture Is Necessary for Low-Cost Food

Sarah Muirhead

Sarah Muirhead is the publisher and editor of Feedstuffs, *a magazine that provides news, information, and analysis on topics related to food production.*

Companion animals are becoming cherished family members and are increasingly included in family-related activities, such as pet Halloween trick-and-treat festivities and happy hours. Animal rights/welfare experts, such as Wes Jamison of the University of Florida, . . . are concerned with this trend and believe it is leading to a growing disconnect between animal agriculture and society in regard to the role of all animals in everyday life. The lines between animals as a source of protein and animals for companionship have become quite blurred, said Jamison.

In Jamison's view, a tectonic shift has happened, and the animal and people worlds have collided. Playing off the popular book [*Men Are from Mars, Woman Are from Venus*], he said it has gotten to the point where animal agriculture is from Mars and animal rights activists are from Venus, and neither understands each other very well.

In the case of animal agriculture, Jamison said, it is basically a situation of not being heard or understood. He said this is largely because consumers no longer have the historic knowledge of why meat, milk and eggs are produced the way they are. Consumers simply fail to equate confinement production with greater efficiency at the production level and, in turn, lower costs at the grocery store. This is particularly in-

Sarah Muirhead, "Lines Blurred on Animals' Role: A Widening Disconnect Between Animal Agriculture and Consumers Is a Growing Concern and, If Not Properly and Promptly Addressed, Could Result in a National Food Security Issue," *Feedstuffs*, vol. 78, December 4, 2006, p. 9. Copyright © 2006 Miller Publishing Company, Inc. Reproduced by permission.

teresting, he said, because consumers are indeed demanding the best of both worlds: low-cost and high-quality food products.

Out of necessity to meet the demands of low-cost but high-quality food production, today's agriculture is driven by a need to rationalize its process whereby minimum inputs are applied to achieve maximum output. Jamison referred to modern animal agriculture as a commodity production business in which the application of good animal welfare leads to good maximum productivity. Consumers need to understand that it is in the best interest of livestock and poultry producers to adhere to sound, science-based animal welfare practices.

Small Island in a Big Sea

In addition to the disconnect with consumers on general production practices, Jamison said another issue complicating the matter is that animal agriculture makes up a very, very small island surrounded by an extensive urban sea. For 50 years, the focus has been on the production of food and fiber, so when something happens in the water around animal agriculture's island, there is little effort made to minimize those initial ripples to keep the larger waves from forming, he said.

Jamison used the example of how, in 1996, the Humane Society of the United States openly stated that its mission was to abolish animal agriculture. At that time, the ripples in the water were starting, but animal agriculture simply kept its sights focused on producing food and fiber rather than countering the emerging opposition. As is evident with recent legislative issues at state and federal levels, left unattended, those ripples in the urban sea have turned into waves.

So, why is legislation being passed affecting how animal agriculture operates and consumers increasingly dictating how their meat, milk and eggs are produced? Jamison explained that a simple look at pet ownership trends provides some good insight:

- More than 80% of U.S. households have two or more nonhuman companions that are viewed as life partners;

- Pets are considered family; and

- In some cases, people say they are closer to their pets than to other family members, including their spouses.

This is exactly why legislation was recently passed in Arizona banning the use of sow gestation crates and in Michigan banning dove hunting, Jamison said. Referencing an Ohio State University study, he said 81% of consumers believe the well-being of farm animals is as important as the well-being of a pet, and 75% feel farm animals should be protected from feeling physical pain.

Consumers simply no longer view food-producing animals as a source of protein but, rather, are projecting their values, desires and needs onto all animals.

All said, the question in consumers' minds has basically switched from "Why animal rights?" to "Why not animal rights?" Jamison said consumers simply no longer view food-producing animals as a source of protein but, rather, are projecting their values, desires and needs onto all animals. Our urbanized society's relationship with animals has changed, and as a result, "Mars and Venus have collided," said Jamison. Consumers equate pigs and chickens with their companion animals and fail to realize that the purpose of production animals is to provide a source of nutrition.

The good news, according to Jamison, is that throughout history, no society has successfully abolished animal agriculture. Nevertheless, he said, U.S. animal agriculture is going to have to get out in front of and pay attention to those shifts or be overwhelmed by them. Everyone involved in the industry—at any level—needs to start talking about the whys of what they do and how that leads to the production of low-cost, high-quality meat, milk and eggs.

Likewise, Jamison said, animal agriculture needs to continuously make sure everything it does is done in a way it can be proud of. If animal agriculture sits back and continues to let the urbanization ripples grow around it, the history of western culture will likely repeat itself, and society will simply decide to export the consequences of its ethical dilemma related to animal production and import its meat, milk and eggs from elsewhere in the world, where the value of animal production is accepted and understood. Jamison explained that such a scenario could well result in food security issues for the U.S.

What You Do and Why You Do It

Here's the point for animal agriculture: The message is to start talking about what you do and why you do it. Get the word out that the U.S. food supply is abundant, low cost and of the highest quality and is so largely because of the production and business practices employed. For the food service sector: Recognize that there are two sides to the story, and strive to educate consumers on the facts so they can make informed food purchasing decisions. For consumers: Recognize that today's modern agriculture provides the best of both worlds: low-cost and high-quality meat, milk and eggs. Be aware that if animal agriculture is outsourced to another country so we, as a society, don't have to "deal with it," both of those assurances could quickly disappear along with the security of the U.S. food supply.

Caging Chickens Protects Them from Avian Flu

Lynne Miller

Lynne Miller is a writer and former editor for Supermarket News, *a weekly trade magazine for the food distribution industry.*

Contrary to what the animal rights advocates say, there's a lot to be said for locking hens up in cages, officials with an egg producers group told SN [*Supermarket News*]. What many people don't realize is modern confinement systems offer a measure of protection against deadly bird flu, said Jeff Armstrong, the dean of the College of Agriculture and Natural Resources at Michigan State University and chairman of the United Egg Producers' [UEP's] Scientific Advisory Committee. "The way to prevent bird flu is to limit contact between wild and domestic birds," said Armstrong, who chaired UEP's Animal Welfare Advisory Committee. "It's frustrating when some animal protection groups that have an agenda to remove animal products say confined egg laying facilities will spread bird flu."

The United States does not have the type of avian influenza strain that's cropped up in Asia and Europe, and industry officials credit the standard practice of housing poultry indoors under strict biosecurity procedures and surveillance for preventing the spread of AI [avian influenza]. Nevertheless, conventional farming practices have taken a beating from animal rights groups.

In [2005], groups succeeded in lobbying retailers and universities to stop selling eggs from caged birds. A premium, niche category, cage-free eggs are gaining mainstream appeal with consumers who support animal rights. [Gourmet market chain] Trader Joe's most recently announced plans to stop selling eggs from caged birds under its private label. Earlier, [health food supermarket chain] Wild Oats Markets agreed to stop carrying eggs from caged birds in all of its stores.

The UEP engaged a public relations firm to communicate the positive side of farm production, and the science-based animal care guidelines under which hens are raised. UEP was instrumental in developing the United Egg Producers Certified program for cage egg production. The program was developed out of guidelines which set standards that protect the comfort, health and safety of chickens, including increased space per hen, standards for beak trimming and maintenance of fresh feed and water. The Food Marketing Institute and National Council of Chain Restaurants have endorsed the guidelines. "We don't have the dollars to do massive advertising," said Gene Gregory, vice president of UEP. "With limited resources, we're trying to get the message out."

About 98% of all the eggs produced in the United States come from farms with modern cage production systems in housing that protects the flock from contact with migratory birds, predators and other diseases, officials at UEP said. Worldwide, more than 90% of eggs are produced in cages.

These people as farmers care about their animals.

"Our producers will produce eggs in whatever form their customers want them in," Gregory said. "Given a choice, because this is their livelihood, they would prefer to produce eggs in cages under this UEP certified program," he said. "Unless you're exclusively cage-free, the opinion of those with multiple systems is they're providing better care for their birds in cage systems than any other system. I can't stress enough [that] these people as farmers care about their animals," he said. "They're interested in the birds' welfare."

Niche Market for Cage-Free Eggs

The cage-free trend is small enough that it hasn't had much of an economic impact on conventional egg producers, he said. For all the recent hoopla over specialty eggs, they don't always carry their weight around the supermarket. Conventionally produced eggs turn much faster than higher-priced specialty eggs at retail, Gregory said, referring to a 2005 report on egg sales.

Still, the growing interest in cage-free eggs has prompted farmers interested in boosting their returns to explore cage-free operations, which are costlier to run. UEP's members include farmers with caged and cage-free operations. "There is increased (producer) interest in cage-free and organic," Gregory acknowledged. "Those are niche markets. They make good money on those."

Free-Range Farms Will Not Stop Farm Animals' Suffering

Lee Hall

Lee Hall is legal director of Friends of Animals, an animal rights advocacy group based in New York.

"Animal agriculture," advocates tell us, "accounts for 98 percent of all animal suffering and killing." What does "all animal suffering and killing" mean? Lawyers David Wolfson and Mariann Sullivan tell us more specifically that farm animals make up 98 percent of all animals "with whom humans interact in the United States."

This 98 percent figure is a cue: Read on, and you'll likely find a discussion of squalid warehouses crammed full of miserable beings. Next, you'll read that most farm animals are virtually invisible to federal law. And finally, because any efficiency is justified in mass production, advocates will often urge support for traditional farming and cage-free eggs.

Yes, animal factories display an obscene disregard for the interests of any conscious beings caught up in their soulless venture. But it makes little sense to try to replace them with supposedly less offensive business practices such as free-range farms.

Here's a reality check: US corporations annually process over eight billion chickens. Add over 100 million pigs, and about 40 million cattle, calves, sheep and lambs. The total number of fish raised for human consumption is in the billions. In order to provide quality of life for the cattle and sheep and chickens, we'd have to clear any remaining national parks and forests, and then invade several more countries.

Rather than point out bluntly that our animal "interactions" have gotta go, non-profit advocacy groups lavish money

Lee Hall, "Animal Rights, Untamed," *Dissident Voice*, March 3, 2006. Reproduced by permission of www.dissidentvoice.org and author.

on campaigns that suggest farm animals can be treated more like pets. Only their naïveté is uncaged. Free-range production, by its very nature, could never be affordable to most of humanity; nor could the planet endure all that methane and manure. And as they push their ill-advised and expensive plans, advocacy groups become consultants to agribusiness. Their employees commit to memory the dimensions of cages, the mechanics of slaughter. What's gained from this?

Animal welfare laws, even where they could fit, would extend no kindnesses to animals where doing so would substantially cut into profit. And no matter what regulations apply to slaughter, at the bottom line, dead means dead.

Reining in the Activists

Animal-welfare advocacy largely functions to ensure that activists conform to the received social and economic template. It transforms activists into paid, staid professionals who negotiate with a few companies over the caging and killing of the animals we commodify, the animals we use. These professionals select videos and reports for publicity value, then find decision-makers who are willing to negotiate, or at least to add pious phrases like "animal compassion" to the corporate and legislative lexicon. And although the reporters who discuss these campaigns use the terms "animal welfare" and "animal-rights" interchangeably, professional welfare lobbying does not advance animal rights. It agrees instead to elaborately codify the human right to use other animals, and commodified animals will always be rightless. That's what it means to be property.

Throughout the advancement of bigger, better confinement and healthy, sustainable animals, free-living animals are continually pushed to the outermost edges of habitable terrain. Professional campaigners relegate *animal rights* to the margins of activism just as they relegate the *animals who can have rights* to the margins of the globe. While they focus on goals such as "improving the living and dying conditions" of animals sold as fast food, they let the interests of free animals languish and become invisible. Yet if free-living animals were thought to have a claim to their territory and freedom, then finally, finally, the polluting and resource-consuming ranchers and animal farmers would meet a true challenge! Animal-welfare advocacy deals only with symptoms, in contrast, and will do so infinitely, without ever challenging our permission to use animals.

If Campaigners Got Serious

If campaigners got serious, they'd have to implicate their colleagues and partners. Question revered family traditions. Pause to reflect on the content of their refrigerators. That's the work of putting animal-rights theory into action; and no, it hasn't a thing to do with making threats or using force. It involves a commitment to *avoid* violence—a far more radical proposal.

The most difficult, often the loneliest, and yet ultimately the most meaningful activism involves the local vegetarian or humane society.

Let me illustrate this. I was recently invited to speak by the animal law section of a state bar association. Compilations of the panelists' work were published. Notices went out to lawyers, students, and activists, announcing such heady topics as defending civil and criminal cases and the effect of the Patriot Act on animal activism. Legal education credits were arranged. PowerPoint technology was in place, as was a collection of gifts for the speakers. The one thing no organizer had assured was that the products of animal agriculture wouldn't be spread across the back table.

My question about breakfast drew sympathy, then impatience. The caterers, I heard, couldn't modify the normal routine. I offered to buy the food, to no avail. This carried on for three days. Finally I decided to refuse to speak in the room. The day before the event, one of the organizers sent me an e-mail: Somebody fixed it.

Then there's the much vaunted "seafood boycott" to rid Newfoundland of its annual seal massacre. If the humane experts and snow-suited militants understood advocacy as meaningfully implicating the habits of their own communities, they would never have buddied up with [natural food store chain] Whole Foods Market and conjured up a seafood boycott to be turned off and on depending on the Canadian government's quota for seal pelts. A holistic intervention (rather than a spectacle) means that we're as respectful of marine life and the marine ecology as we expect the Canadian coast-dwellers to be. And because a holistic intervention would view Newfoundlanders as potential allies, it would exert its economic pressure not on the people living as near to the poverty line as to the sea, but on the government that sets the quotas, opens new markets, and fails to engage the human potential of its coastal populace.

The point of an animal-rights movement isn't to narrowly tailor angst to whatever seems crude and barbaric, preferably done by foreigners. The most difficult, often the loneliest, and yet ultimately the most meaningful activism involves the local vegetarian or humane society or the sing-along at the peace café. The cream in the coffee might seem, to some, unworthy of political action, but the milk of the mothers of others is a good place to begin to interrogate our universal domination of other conscious beings—indeed, the idea of domination itself. In the cream, we see the experience of a cow whose life consists of pregnancies and separations and whose death is violent, and if animal-rights activism means anything, it involves that cream, that product of deforestation that ruins the earth for animals who could have enjoyed a life of freedom. The cream in the coffee connects us with the polluted streams and the pesticides that poison workers and the land.

Students Essential to Activism

After we weather the tempests in our own teapots, we can pressure our universities and municipalities to disengage from the promotion of dairy and flesh products. Students can be an essential part of this community activism; but so far we find students acting like salespeople. After meeting with the campus "animal rights" group, the University of Connecticut recently agreed to buy Certified Humane Raised and Handled eggs. The campus newspaper explained: "Some students have been vocal in the pursuit of a dining facility that follows a 'farm-to-fork' philosophy, emphasizing humane treatment of animals and minimal processing." The new eggs cost double what the old eggs did, but the dining hall's assistant manager is delighted with the new, improved oval reproductive morsels: The banana bread is now "lighter and fluffier" and students "seem to be eating more eggs just to try them out."

When several school cafeterias in Washington, D.C. made similar moves, the Humane Society of the United States praised the trend. The Baltimore Animal Rights Coalition carried the news to suburban Sterling and Fairfax, Virginia, advertising the "conditions in which animals live and die on factory farms" and pressing Wegmans to "join its competitors Whole Foods, Wild Oats and Trader Joe's"—groceries that already stock the connoisseur-class eggs.

I hope the reader will wonder why the advocates don't simply recommend that people refrain from egg shopping. I wonder myself. I presume that they've become accustomed to wielding the leverage that's the privilege of consumers. Being players.

The free-range label appeals to shoppers who see factory farms as inhumane, uncouth, or biologically dangerous. For investors in this sector, profits can be impressive. Britain's latest figures, out last month [February 2006], show that the value of non-cage egg sales has overtaken cage-produced eggs. Even McDonald's uses free-range eggs these days. And at

Zuma, over the road from Harrod's of London, customers pay £55 ($96) for a Wagyu burger—the ground flesh of cows that were once given massages and beer on New Zealand grass.

Activism is meaningless unless it champions a lifestyle free of animal products.

Most "free-range" offerings are, in reality, mass-produced commodities involving no pastures at all. The egg and dairy industries are notorious for their overall treatment, and the few cast-offs living in sanctuaries were typically found starved, neglected or abused—common situations for animals raised for human consumption, including on so-called family farms.

Showing Animal Agribusiness the Door

So the animal-rights revolution will not be found on the farm. Even when advocates do intervene for free-living animals, activism is meaningless unless it champions a lifestyle free of animal products. Notably, militant groups that condemn meat eating still leave dairy and eggs up to the activist. Then, still ambivalent about boycotting animal agribusiness, the militants set off to release and rescue animals.

Little if anything changes after a private act of rescue. The laws protecting the industries become stricter, but demand does not change. Radical activism would mean going to the root of the problem, dissuading the public from supporting animal agribusiness. A firebomb can't do that any better than an undercover video showing violations of the Animal Welfare Act. These aren't radical acts. Contrary to an increasingly popular belief, making oneself and others vulnerable to law enforcement doesn't make anyone radical. Offering oneself as raw material to the prison industry supports the makers of cages. In a world where coercion has, for so long, been the tedious norm, truly radical activism seeks and models a view in which respect prevails.

No one can be arrested for buying eggless noodles. Yet setting oneself free from the social addiction to animal products is serious direct action. It's not a matter of decrying the worst abuses—agriculture's torture photos—but of challenging the appalling communal injustices of the everyday. At a time when corporations have legal personhood, yet the conscious individuals used as raw materials do not, no activism can be more basic, more direct, or more needed.

Hesitance Is Born of Fear

And it's difficult. Even the people at your peace marches and your progressive book readings will deny a radical idea when it implicates lunch. Don't alienate people, you'll be told. Everyone must travel at their own pace along the path. I believe this hesitance is born of fear, and that it goes back a long way. People still associate survival with fighting and vanquishing; just look at children's cartoons and the old fear is there. We *homo sapiens* are an insecure lot. We're all still fighting and vanquishing animals by deliberately ignoring the unremitting destruction of their territory. By ignoring their numbers when they fall in the wars we wage. By the deforestation of their habitat and the expansion of our farming. By only permitting them to exist insofar as we can take advantage of them as tourist attractions, experimental subjects, film props, guards, playthings, or something to package in bright yellow foam and unwrap, ingest, and excrete.

Free-Range Does Not Challenge

The free-range notion doesn't challenge any of it. It injects an incoherent sort of flexibility into people who'd otherwise be drawn to vegetarian ideals. But professional welfare advocacy hasn't come for ideals; it's come for bargaining power. The sprawling welfare administrations could never pressure multinational corporations, or make high-profile agreements and expand their sphere of influence and grow their millions in various banks if their members were vegetarians. So they become gatekeepers, experts on how to handle the 98% of animals with whom we interact.

Animal rights is only a viable idea as long as there is an animal world at liberty to avoid such interactions. We think of the future for wolves, for caribou, for nectar bats, pronghorn antelope, Atlantic salmon and sea turtles.

There is a saying that people often somehow resemble the animals with whom they live. Perhaps we could say that people resemble the animals for whom we advocate. Those who advocate for the rights of free-living animals—which are, ultimately, the only animal rights there are—won't be tamed.

A Vegan Lifestyle Is Necessary to Stop the Mistreatment of Animals

Bruce Friedrich

Bruce Friedrich is vice president of International Grassroots Campaigns for People for the Ethical Treatment of Animals (PETA), a well-known animal rights advocacy group.

The ... reason I hear for adopting a vegetarian diet—and this may be the most important reason for teenagers and college students—is the growing understanding that animals feel pain in the same way that we do. In fact, it's this realization, that animals are not automatons, that forms the basis of the modern animal rights movement.

The Right to Be Free from Suffering

Dr. Andrew Linzey, a theologian at Oxford University, points out that animals were designed with certain needs, desires, natural behaviors, and inclinations, just as human beings were, and that animals have the capacity for pain and suffering, just as human beings do.

Other animals are made of flesh, blood, and bone—a dead animal is, like a dead human, a corpse. And animals have the same five physiological senses of sight, smell, hearing, taste, and touch. Their experiences are similar. Any difference between a human and another animal is a difference of degree, not kind. From Linzey's perspective, denying animals the things that they were designed to do and inflicting pain on them for reasons of convenience are categorically unethical. Linzey argues that causing pain to an animal is the moral

Bruce Friedrich, "Vegetarianism in a Nutshell: Animal Rights," People for the Ethical Treatment of Animals (PETA), December 29, 2007. Reproduced by permission. www.goveg.com/veganism_animal.asp.

equivalent of causing pain to a human being, because from the vantage point of the one harmed, the pain is the same.

Basically, Linzey's view is the animal rights perspective. The animal rights perspective holds that animals have a right, just as human beings do, to be free from pain and suffering. Back in the 18th century, Jeremy Bentham, the father of the Utilitarian movement, stated that if we're talking about a being's right to be free from pain and suffering, then the morally relevant variable is not whether that being can think or talk or how we relate to that being's life, but rather his or her capacity to feel pain and to suffer. Of course, any introductory physiology course will teach you that birds, mammals, and fish all have the same basic capacity to suffer. We share this capacity with all animals.

Prejudice is prejudice, whether it is based on race or gender or religion—or on species.

The animal rights movement is a movement for justice, just like the abolition of slavery, suffrage, civil rights, and women's rights. Most people today understand that bias on the basis of race, gender, religion, or nationality—any bias against other human beings—is wrong. Species bias—the idea that just because certain beings are not human, we can do whatever we wish with them—has yet to become widely accepted. Dr. Albert Schweitzer put it well when he stated that "compassion, in which ethics takes root, does not assume its true proportions until it embraces not only man but every living being."

Again, prejudice is prejudice, whether it is based on race or gender or religion—or on species. In each case, a line is drawn, separating those in the group above the line from those in the group below the line. Nobel laureate Isaac Bashevis Singer, who fled Nazi-occupied Poland, compared species bias to the "most extreme racist theories" and thought that animal rights was the purest form of justice advocacy, because animals are the most vulnerable of all the downtrodden. He felt that mistreating animals was the epitome of the "might makes right" moral paradigm—a moral paradigm that is ethically bankrupt.

Interestingly, the animal rights perspective has been embraced by a wide range of brilliant thinkers and humanitarians that includes, in addition to those I've already mentioned, [mathematician] Pythagoras, [artist and inventor] Leonardo da Vinci, [physicist] Albert Einstein, [writer] Harriet Beecher Stowe, [author] C.S. Lewis, [civil rights leader] Susan B. Anthony, [Russian writer] Leo Tolstoy, [comedian] Dick Gregory, and [Indian leader] Mahatma Gandhi.

Veganism the Only Choice

In conclusion, I'm convinced, on the basis of the evidence, that a vegan diet is, without a doubt, the very best choice for our health, the only sustainable choice for the environment, and the only choice that expresses in a positive manner who we are in the world—compassionate people, compassionate toward people and toward animals.

Albert Einstein said that nothing would benefit humanity more than the general adoption of a vegetarian diet. Leo Tolstoy stated, "Vegetarianism is the taproot of humanitarianism." Their point, as they elaborated, is that eating is essential to who we are. There is a lot of suffering in the world. There are a lot of problems. Solutions will require time and devotion from people of goodwill. But if every time we sit down to eat we choose to support animal abuse, unjust human and environmental degradation, what does that say about our integrity, about our commitment to other issues of social justice? Again, according to Tolstoy, "Vegetarianism is the taproot of humanitarianism."

A Historical Perspective

It is interesting to recall that slavery on this continent flourished from the 1620s until the mid-1860s. Women were not given the right to vote in the U.S. until 1920, with the passage of the 19th Amendment. Many people listening probably have close relatives who were alive when there was a spirited debate in Congress about whether the Union would dissolve if these irrational creatures, women, were given a say in governance. One hundred years ago, there wasn't a single law against child abuse in this country. Not one. Your child was your property.

One hundred years ago, there was not a single country on the planet that guaranteed the vote to all adults. It's remarkable to recall that just 350 years ago, the Pope sentenced Galileo to the torture chamber until he would recant the "heresy" that the Earth is not the center of the physical universe.

For a bit of historical perspective here, let's recall that Socrates was teaching 2,600 years ago; Plato and Aristotle were philosophizing 2,500 years ago. Jesus was preaching 2,000 years ago. Shakespeare was writing 500 years ago. But we just got around to saying, "Hey, maybe people shouldn't hold slaves, and maybe people shouldn't be free to beat their children, and maybe women are rational enough to be given a say in governance," fewer than 150 years ago.

I mention all this only to point out how quickly things change. Not long ago, a mere historical blink of an eye, society believed with complete certainty the diametrical opposite of what we believe, and with equal certainty, to be true about many things today.

Look how far the animal rights movement has come in, historically, no time at all. In just the past 20 years, science has shown that a vegan diet is the healthiest and environmental researchers have proved that eating meat, dairy products, and eggs is not sustainable. Even more importantly, the scientific view that animals don't feel emotion has been replaced by a new, belated understanding that, of course, they do. In just the past few years, the issue of animal treatment on factory farms has taken center stage, with the U.S. Congress decrying slaughterhouse treatment of animals, the fast-food giants requiring some improvements for animals, and *The Washington Post* running front page stories about some of the abuses.

The animal rights movement is a movement for justice, just like the abolition of slavery, suffrage, civil rights, and women's rights.

When I became a vegan in 1987, vegetarian foods were just coming on the market, and some didn't taste very good. Now, Silk-brand soy milk is in every grocery store in the country, and even [television] shows like *20/20* are proving, in blind taste tests, that people like it better than cow's milk. Chains like Burger King, Johnny Rockets, and Ruby Tuesday are selling fabulous veggie burgers across the country. Veggie wraps and gourmet salads are more popular than ever. Millions and millions of people are learning that moral integrity requires that when we sit down to eat, we make conscious choices, rather than unconscious ones, and that the only diet for environmentalists, animal lovers, and people who care about their health is a vegan one.

The 18th century saw the beginnings of our democratic system, which was the first to hold that "all men are created equal" and which established, under the law, basic freedoms such as the rights to assemble peacefully, practice one's chosen religion, say what one likes, and print what one likes. The 19th century abolished slavery in the developed world. The 20th century abolished child labor, criminalized child abuse, and gave women the vote and blacks wider rights. If we all do as much as we can, the 21st century *can* be the one for animal rights.

Living One's Values

I suppose for me, it boils down to Socrates' adage from 2600 years ago, "The unexamined life is not worth living." It seems to me that what it means to be a person of integrity is that I try to ask questions, that I try not to support things that I oppose, that I try to make my life mean something.

That's what I think it means to have integrity—that I try to lead a life that is in keeping with my professed values—my opposition to human exploitation, my view of myself as an environmentalist, my desire to be as healthy as possible, so I can work and play harder, my belief in kindness, toward other people and toward animals.

Please ask yourself: "Would you want to work on a factory farm, searing the beaks off of chickens or castrating pigs and cows without painkillers, and so on?" "Would you want to work on a factory fishing trawler?" "Are [there] other areas of your life where you participate in practices that would repulse you if you had to watch them happening?" You know, most of us could watch grains being tilled or even spend an afternoon shucking corn or picking beans, fruits, or vegetables. Seriously, how many of us would want to spend an afternoon slitting open animals' throats?

Any decision to decrease consumption of animal products is to be celebrated, even as it's seen as a step toward the transition to a totally vegan diet.

Some people go vegan overnight; others take a bit more time. I don't want to discount the power that convenience, social pressure, and so on, can wield. Clearly, any decision to decrease consumption of animal products is to be celebrated, even as it's seen as a step toward the transition to a totally vegan diet.

I think that ethics must include living a life that is, as much as possible, in keeping with our basic values. We can't be perfect, but we really should all do as much as we can.

I have no doubt that in 100 years, human beings will look back on the human mistreatment of other animals with the same horror we presently reserve for historical injustices such as slavery and moral transgressions against human beings.

Animals suffer and die like we do. Animals are made of the same stuff we are. Eating them is an act of gluttony and disregard for our own health, for the environment, for the global poor, and most of all, for our fellow animals. If you are not a vegan, please work toward becoming one. If you are a vegan, thank you so much for caring and please become more active.

One of the exciting things about helping animals, the Earth, and your own health is that you don't have to fill out a form or make a call. You can start today, by choosing a healthy, humane, vegan meal when you sit down to eat.

CHAPTER 3

Is Animal Medical Experimentation Justified?

Chapter Overview: The Animal Experimentation Debate

Simon Festing

Dr. Simon Festing is the executive director of the Research Defense Society.

The European Union is about to publish a revised draft of the law that governs animal experiments across Europe. Our vision is that Europe and the UK should remain world leaders in advanced biomedical research which will allow us to develop new medicines to save lives and alleviate the suffering of millions of people. A small but vital part of that research will involve the use of animals.

The last decade has seen intense controversy about animal experiments in the UK. Much of the debate in the national media has been highly polarised. There is genuine public concern about the well-being of animals used for research. But at the same time there is strong public support for properly and humanely conducted medical research using animals. In the review of European laws, we see an opportunity for a more sophisticated debate.

A number of expert committees in the UK have published detailed reports on animal research, including a House of Lords Select Committee, a government advisory committee, and the respected Nuffield Council on Bioethics. They have all backed well-regulated research, but have called for more informed debate and greater efforts to replace and reduce the use of animals in research. There are signs of progress already. As well as having the most comprehensive laws to protect animals, the UK now produces more information about animal research than any other country in the world—through the publication on the Home Office website of summary information about animal research projects.

Although many medical advances are still likely to depend to some extent on animal-based research, we must recognise that animals can and do suffer in research. This will always raise difficult ethical issues. Alternative methods should be used when available, and the best regulatory system to protect animals is essential. Animal welfare standards must be high, and animals should be well treated and used in minimum numbers.

The UK government has responded sensibly to the debate about animal research. It has set up a new organisation called the National Centre for the 3Rs which will help find ways to reduce the numbers of animals used, to replace the use of animals with alternatives, and to ensure that any experiments are refined to minimise suffering to the animals (the 'three Rs').

Where there is no alternative to using animals, we must also find ways of improving the results from animal studies, through better design and analysis of the experiments, and through advances in science and technology.

There has been much debate in recent years about the extent to which we really need to use animals in research. A number of leading scientific organisations have outlined ways in which we can bring forward methods to replace and reduce animal use. Vast investments are being made in non-animal techniques which will help to achieve these objectives.

But where there is no alternative to using animals, we must also find ways of improving the results from animal studies, through better design and analysis of the experiments, and through advances in science and technology.

Benefits of Animal Research

In the short term, we have to recognise an inescapable truth. The number of animals used in research is going to go up. This is partly because the use of genetically modified animals allows us to study the underlying basis of diseases in a more powerful way. It is also because new and sophisticated medicines are being developed which can target diseases more effectively. An example is the medicine Herceptin which was not only discovered and tested in mice, but actually comes from mice. It saves the lives of many women with breast cancer.

None of this will stop the onslaught from vitriolic animal rights groups, who continue to claim that animal research does not work and that scientists go to work every day to abuse animals. They presumably are talking about the fish, rats and mice which make up the vast majority of animals used. These absurd arguments have no credibility and should be ignored. We need to address the far more important issues outlined above, especially continuing to improve how we care for and use animals across all research centres in Europe. It is time to get away from the polarised debate, and face the real ethical and scientific challenges of tomorrow.

Human Well-Being Requires the Use of Animals for Medical Research

Alex Epstein

Alex Epstein is a junior fellow at the Irvine, California, office of the Ayn Rand Institute, a nonprofit think tank.

The "animal rights" movement has pulled off a deadly deception: promote a vicious, anti-human policy while feigning benevolent, compassionate motives. The deception takes the form of opposing lifesaving medical research—in the name of opposing cruelty to animals.

A Classic Smear Campaign

Consider People for the Ethical Treatment of Animals' [PETA] ongoing campaign against Princeton, N.J.–based Covance, a company that conducts vital medical research on animals to fight diseases such as breast cancer, diabetes and Alzheimer's. PETA is staging an elaborate, heavily backed PR [public relations] effort claiming that Covance engages in gratuitous and unnecessary torture of monkeys. The centerpiece of the campaign is a five-minute video allegedly proving PETA's accusations.

In fact, PETA's effort is a classic smear campaign. Many of the "abuses" it documents—such as the use of restraints or delivering drugs through nasal tubes—are necessary to effectively administer drugs to animals. And the few examples of seemingly inappropriate behavior they find, such as the bizarre taunting of monkeys by a few Covance employees, are treated as pervasive industry practice—even though it took a

Alex Epstein, "Animal Rights Movement Is Cruelty to Humans," *San Diego Business Journal*, vol. 26, August 22, 2005, pp. 46–47. Copyright © 2005 San Diego Business Journal Associates. All rights reserved. Reproduced by permission.

PETA operative (operating illegally within Covance) more than 10 months to cull a mere handful of such instances.

Animal research is absolutely necessary for the development of lifesaving drugs, medical procedures and biotech treatments.

No sane person seeks to inflict needless pain on animals. Such practices, where they exist, should be condemned. But anyone concerned for human life must unequivocally endorse the rightness of using animals in medical research.

Animal research is absolutely necessary for the development of lifesaving drugs, medical procedures and biotech treatments. According to Nobel laureate Dr. Joseph Murray, "Animal experimentation has been essential to the development of all cardiac surgery, transplantation surgery, joint replacements and all vaccinations." Explains former American Medical Association President Dr. Daniel Johnson, "Animal research—followed by human clinical study—is absolutely necessary to find the causes and cures for so many deadly threats, from AIDS to cancer."

Millions of humans would suffer and die unnecessarily if animal testing were prohibited. But this is exactly what PETA and other "animal rights" organizations seek. They believe that all animal research should be banned, including research conducted as humanely as possible (the declared and scrupulously practiced policy of most animal researchers).

Sacrificing Human Well-Being

The founder of PETA, Ingrid Newkirk, has declared unequivocally that animal research is "immoral even if it's essential" and that "even painless research is fascism, supremacism." When questioned what her movement's stance would be if animal tests produced a cure for AIDS, Newkirk responded, "We'd be against it." Chris DeRose, founder of the group Last

Chance for Animals, writes, "If the death of one rat cured all diseases, it wouldn't make any difference to me."

The goal of the "animal rights" movement is not to stop sadistic animal torturers; it is to sacrifice human well-being for the sake of animals. This goal is inherent in the very notion of "animal rights." According to PETA, the basic principle of "animal rights" is: "animals are not ours to eat, wear, experiment on, or use for entertainment"—they "deserve consideration of their own best interests regardless of whether they are useful to humans."

Protecting Human Interests

This is in exact contradiction to the requirements of human survival and progress, which demand that we kill animals when they endanger us, eat them when we need food and run tests on them to fight disease. To ascribe rights to animals is to contradict the purpose and justification of rights: the protection of human interests.

Rights are moral principles governing the interactions of rational, productive beings, who prosper not in a world of eat or be eaten, but a world of voluntary, mutually beneficial cooperation and trade. The death and destruction that would result from any serious attempt to pretend that animals have rights would be catastrophic—for humans—a prospect the movement's most consistent members embrace. Newkirk calls human beings "the biggest blight on the face of the Earth."

Millions of humans would suffer and die unnecessarily if animal testing were prohibited.

The central issue in the "animal rights" debate is not whether it is acceptable to torture animals, but whether it is proper to use them for human benefit. The "animal rights" movement's emphasis on the senseless torture of animals—in the rare cases where it actually exists—is a red herring. It is a way of promoting opposition to lifesaving animal research companies, and sympathy for themselves—so as to further their evil agenda of subjugating human beings to animals. They must not be allowed to get away with such dishonesty. What is needed is a principled, intellectual defense of the absolute right of animal experimentation, against the deadly notion of "animal rights." Anything less is cruelty to humans.

Animals Should Not Be Given Rights at the Expense of Human Needs

Edwin A. Locke

Edwin A. Locke is a professor at the University of Maryland in College Park and a senior writer for the Ayn Rand Institute, an organization that promotes the ideas of Ayn Rand, the originator of a philosophy called Objectivism.

Human life versus animal life. This fundamental conflict of values, which was dramatized a few years ago when AIDS victims marched in support of research on animals, is still raging. [In 2005] PETA (People for the Ethical Treatment of Animals) launched a campaign against Covance, Inc., a biomedical research lab in Vienna, Va., that uses animals for drug testing.

It is an indisputable fact that many thousands of lives are saved by medical research on animals. But animal rightists don't care. PETA makes this frighteningly clear: "Even if animal tests produced a cure for AIDS, we'd be against it." Such is the "humanitarianism" of animal rights activists.

The Invalid Animal Rights Argument

How do these advocates try to justify their position? As someone who has debated them for years on college campuses and in the media, I know firsthand that the whole movement is based on a single—invalid—syllogism, namely: men feel pain and have rights; animals feel pain; therefore, animals have rights. This argument is entirely specious, because man's rights do not depend on his ability to feel pain; they depend on his ability to think.

Edwin A. Locke, "Animal 'Rights' Versus Human Rights," *Intellectual Conservative*, June 2, 2005. Reproduced by permission. www.intellectualconservative.com/article4376.html.

Rights are ethical principles applicable only to beings capable of reason and choice. There is only one fundamental right: a man's right to his own life. To live successfully, man must use his rational faculty—which is exercised by choice. The choice to think can be negated only by the use of physical force. To survive and prosper, men must be free from the initiation of force by other men—free to use their own minds to guide their choices and actions. Rights protect men against the use of force by other men.

To claim that man's use of animals is immoral . . . is to elevate amoral animals to a moral level higher than ourselves—a flagrant contradiction.

None of this is relevant to animals. Animals do not survive by rational thought (nor by sign languages allegedly taught to them by psychologists). They survive through sensory-perceptual association and the pleasure-pain mechanism. They cannot reason. They cannot learn a code of ethics. A lion is not immoral for eating a zebra (or even for attacking a man). Predation is their natural and only means of survival; they do not have the capacity to learn any other.

Rights are ethical principles applicable only to beings capable of reason and choice.

Only man has the power, guided by a code of morality, to deal with other members of his own species by voluntary means: rational persuasion. To claim that man's use of animals is immoral is to claim that we have no right to our own lives and that we must sacrifice our welfare for the sake of creatures who cannot think or grasp the concept of morality. It is to elevate amoral animals to a moral level higher than ourselves—a flagrant contradiction. Of course, it is proper not to cause animals gratuitous suffering. But this is not the same as inventing a bill of rights for them—at our expense.

Animal Advocates Hate Humans

The granting of fictional rights to animals is not an innocent error. We do not have to speculate about the motive, because the animal "rights" advocates have revealed it quite openly. Again from PETA: "Mankind is the biggest blight on the face of the earth"; "I do not believe that a human being has a right to life"; "I would rather have medical experiments done on our children than on animals." These self-styled lovers of life do not love animals; rather, they hate men.

The animal "rights" terrorists are like the Unabomber and Oklahoma City bombers[1] They are not idealists seeking justice, but nihilists seeking destruction for the sake of destruction. They do not want to uplift mankind, to help him progress from the swamp to the stars. They want mankind's destruction; they want him not just to stay in the swamp but to disappear into its muck.

There is only one proper answer to such people: to declare proudly and defiantly, in the name of morality, a man's right to his life, his liberty, and the pursuit of his own happiness.

1. The Unabomber, Theodore John Kaczynski, carried out a series of bombings and letter bombings from the late 1970s to the mid-1990s that killed three people and wounded twenty-three; the Oklahoma City bombing was a domestic terrorist attack on the Alfred P. Murrah Federal Building on April 19, 1995, carried out by Timothy McVeigh and Terry Nichols.

Mistreatment of Animals by Researchers Is Rare

Tom Still

Tom Still is president of the Wisconsin Technology Council and the former associate editor of the Wisconsin State Journal.

A t one level, it's possible to understand why animal-rights advocates passionately oppose experiments involving animals. No one likes to see another creature suffer needlessly. Beyond the passion, however, exist facts about animal-based research that run counter to the intimidating tactics of some protesters, such as those who . . . targeted the homes of researchers in Madison [Wisconsin]. Information about the true extent of animal research—and its benefits for humans and animals alike—deserves to be heard above the bullhorns and protest signs.

The Value of Animal Research

Our quality of life has been improved significantly by biological research that sometimes relies on the use of animals in controlled experiments. A generation or more of people has never known what it was like to be unable to swim in the summer for fear of contracting polio, to go blind or deaf because of infections, or to expect that any cancer diagnosis was a death sentence.

Animal-based research has helped provide cures and treatments in those cases and many more. Biotechnology companies have depended on animal research to develop more than 160 drugs and vaccines approved by the U.S. Food and Drug Administration, according to the Biotechnology Industry Organization. Those discoveries have helped hundreds of millions of people worldwide and prevented incalculable human suffering.

In addition, . . . animal research has led to 111 USDA [U.S. Department of Agriculture] approved biotech-derived veterinary biologics and vaccines that improve the health of livestock, poultry and companion animals. Biotech veterinary products to treat heartworm, arthritis, parasites, allergies and heart disease, as well as vaccines for rabies and feline HIV, are used daily by veterinarians. Biotechnology has improved the way veterinarians address animal health issues through the use of biotech vaccines and diagnostic kits and improved breeding programs that can help to eliminate hereditary diseases.

All of this has been accomplished amid an array of government regulation and researcher self-policing that has made examples of animal mistreatment rare. At UW-Madison [University of Wisconsin], the All-Campus Animal Care and Use Committee functions as an oversight body for all animal use. Such institutional bodies are required by the U.S. Department of Agriculture and the federal Animal Welfare Act.

Animals used in research do not suffer more pain or distress than animals outside the lab. In fact, lab animals often receive the best of care.

The USDA and National Institutes of Health regularly inspect research institutions to verify the well-being and care of animals. With very few exceptions that serve as rallying points for advocates, animals used in research do not suffer more pain or distress than animals outside the lab. In fact, lab animals often receive the best of care because of their value to researchers.

Today, animal research is predominantly research involving rodents and rabbits. At GlaxoSmithKline PLC's London division, for example, only 5 percent of research and development involves animals—and 99 percent of those animals are mice, rats and rabbits. Protesters may flash disturbing images of monkeys screaming in pain, but primates aren't at the core of most animal research today.

Computer modeling has reduced the amount of animal research. So has cell-based research. The use of animal embryonic stem cells in drug testing has dramatically improved the quality of such tests, and more quickly provided researchers with information about the safety and efficacy of drugs.

Safe, Humane Research

In the future, use of human embryonic stem cells in drug testing could further reduce the use of animals in testing. Perhaps it is time for animal-rights groups to redirect some of their energy to standing up for human stem cell research.

For now and well into the future, animal testing will be a part of scientific research. That research is being conducted safely and humanely by researchers who are dedicated to finding cures for some of mankind's worst diseases—as well as conditions that plague animals themselves. Don't let rare cases of cruelty to research animals drive public opinion about a practice that helps humans and animals alike.

The Value of Animal Experimentation Is Exaggerated

Christopher Anderegg, Kathy Archibald, Jarrod Bailey, Murry J. Cohen, Stephen R. Kaufman, and John J. Pippin

Christopher Anderegg, Kathy Archibald, Jarrod Bailey, Murry J. Cohen, Stephen R. Kaufman, and John J. Pippin are members of the Medical Research Modernization Committee, a nonprofit health advocacy organization that promotes efficient, cost-effective, and reliable research methods.

Increasing numbers of scientists and clinicians are challenging animal experimentation on medical and scientific grounds. . . . Considerable evidence demonstrates that animal experimentation is inefficient and unreliable, while newly developed methodologies are more valid and less expensive than animal studies.

Proponents of animal experimentation (tests, experiments and "educational" exercises involving harm to animals) claim that it has played a crucial role in virtually all medical advances. However, several medical historians argue that key discoveries in such areas as heart disease, cancer, immunology, anesthesia and psychiatry were in fact achieved through clinical research, observation of patients and human autopsy.

Human data has historically been interpreted in light of laboratory data derived from nonhuman animals. This has resulted in unfortunate medical consequences. For instance, by 1963 prospective and retrospective studies of human patients had already shown a strong correlation between cigarette smoking and lung cancer. In contrast, almost all experimental

Christopher Anderegg, Kathy Archibald, Jarrod Bailey, Murry J. Cohen, Stephen R. Kaufman, John J. Pippin, "A Critical Look at Animal Experimentation," Shaker Heights, OH: Medical Research Modernization Committee, 2006. © Medical Research Modernization Committee, 2006. Reproduced by permission. www.mrmcmed.org/Critical_Look.pdf.

efforts to produce lung cancer in animals had failed. As a result, Clarence Little, a leading cancer animal experimenter, wrote: "The failure of many investigators to induce experimental cancers, except in a handful of cases, during fifty years of trying, casts serious doubt on the validity of the cigarette-lung cancer theory." Because the human and animal data failed to agree, this researcher and others distrusted the more reliable human data. As a result, health warnings were delayed for years, while thousands of people died of lung cancer.

Many other important medical advances have been delayed because of misleading information derived from animal "models."

By the early 1940s, human clinical investigation strongly indicated that asbestos causes cancer. However, animal studies repeatedly failed to demonstrate this, and proper workplace precautions were not instituted in the U.S. until decades later. Similarly, human population studies have shown a clear risk from exposure to low-level ionizing radiation from diagnostic X-rays and nuclear wastes, but contradictory animal studies have stalled proper warnings and regulations. Likewise, while the connection between alcohol consumption and cirrhosis [a liver disease] is indisputable in humans, repeated efforts to produce cirrhosis by excessive alcohol ingestion have failed in all nonhuman animals except baboons, and even the baboon data is inconsistent.

Medical Advances Delayed

Many other important medical advances have been delayed because of misleading information derived from animal "models." The animal model of polio, for example, resulted in a misunderstanding of the mechanism of infection. Studies on monkeys falsely indicated that the polio virus was transmitted via a respiratory, rather than a digestive route. This erroneous assumption resulted in misdirected preventive measures and delayed the development of tissue culture methodologies critical to the discovery of a vaccine. While monkey cell cultures were later used for vaccine production, it was research with human cell cultures which first showed that the polio virus could be cultivated on non-neural tissue. Similarly, development of surgery to replace clogged arteries with the patient's own veins was impeded by dog experiments which falsely indicated that veins could not be used. Likewise, kidney transplants, quickly rejected in healthy dogs, were accepted for a much longer time in human patients. We now know that kidney failure suppresses the immune system, which increases tolerance of foreign tissues.

In addition to squandering scarce resources and providing misleading results, animal experimentation poses real risks to humans.

Nevertheless, society continues to support animal experimentation, primarily because many people believe that it has been vital for most medical advances. However, few question whether such research has been necessary or even beneficial to medical progress.

In addition to squandering scarce resources and providing misleading results, animal experimentation poses real risks to humans. The mind-set that scientific knowledge justifies and requires harming innocent individuals endangers all who are vulnerable. Even after Nazi and Japanese experiments on prisoners horrified the world, American researchers denied African-American men syphilis treatment in order to assess the disease's natural progression, they deliberately exposed students and minorities to toxic chemicals in order to determine safe levels of exposure to pesticides, they intentionally exposed thousands of unsuspecting civilians to lethal bacteria in order to test biological warfare, they injected cancer cells into nursing home patients, subjected unwitting patients to dangerous radiation experiments, and, despite no chance of success, transplanted nonhuman primate and pig organs into children, as well as chronically ill and impoverished people. Psychiatrist Robert Jay Lifton argues that this "science at any cost" mentality may have provided medical justification for the Holocaust.

Humans Exposed to Viruses

Furthermore, through animal research, humans have been exposed to a wide variety of deadly nonhuman primate viruses. About 16 laboratory workers have been killed by the Marburg virus and other monkey viruses, and two outbreaks of Ebola have occurred in American monkey colonies. Polio vaccines grown on monkey kidney cells exposed millions of Americans to the simian virus 40, which causes human cells to undergo malignant transformation *in vitro* and has been found in several human cancers. Ignoring the obvious public health hazards, researchers transplanted baboon bone marrow cells into an AIDS patient. The experiment was unsuccessful; moreover, a large number of baboon viruses, which the patient could have spread to other people, may have accompanied the bone marrow. Indeed, animal experimentation may have started the AIDS epidemic. HIV-1, the principal AIDS virus, differs markedly from all other viruses found in nature, and there is evidence that it originated either through polio vaccine production using monkey tissues or through manufacture in American laboratories, where HIV-like viruses were being produced by cancer and biological weapons researchers in the early 1970s.

Failing to learn from the AIDS epidemic, many policy makers and industrial interest groups support animal-to-human organ transplants (from pigs and primates) known as xenotransplants. These have failed in the past and will most likely continue to fail because of tissue rejection, the impossibility of testing animal tissues for unknown pathogens, and the prohibitive expense.

Similarly, the rapidly expanding field of genetic engineering includes adding genetic material to animals' cells to change the animals' growth patterns or induce the animals to produce human proteins in their milk, meat or urine. Harvesting such proteins poses serious human health risks, such as exposure to pathogens (viruses, prions and other microorganisms) or the development of malignancies, allergic reactions or antibiotic resistance. These concerns contributed to the European Union's ban on rBGH, a genetically engineered bovine growth hormone that increases cows' milk production.

Although animal experimentation advocates routinely take credit for discoveries . . . , many clinicians have recognized the primary role of human-based clinical research.

Typically, medical discovery begins with a clinical observation, which animal experimenters then try to mimic with artificially induced conditions in laboratory animals. These researchers tend to highlight animal data that agrees with the previous clinical finding, while discounting or ignoring conflicting animal data. . . . Although animal experimentation advocates routinely take credit for discoveries that actually occurred in a clinical context, many clinicians have recognized the primary role of human-based clinical research. Reviewing the history of hepatitis, physician Paul Beeson concluded: "Progress in the understanding and management of human disease must begin, and end, with studies of man. . . . Hepatitis, although an almost 'pure' example of progress by the study of man, is by no means unusual; in fact, it is more nearly the rule. To cite other examples: appendicitis, rheumatic fever, typhoid fever, ulcerative colitis and hyperparathyroidism." . . .

Furthermore, clinical research is the only means by which effective public health education and prevention programs can be developed and evaluated.

Nonanimal Methods

In science, there are always many ways to address a given question. Animal experimentation is generally less efficient and reliable than many nonanimal methods, which include:

1. Epidemiology (Human Population Studies)

Medical research has always sought to identify the underlying causes of human disease in order to develop effective preventive and therapeutic measures. In contrast to artificial animal model conditions that generally differ in causes and mechanisms from human conditions, human population studies have been very fruitful. For example, the identification of the major risk factors for coronary heart disease, such as smoking, elevated cholesterol and high blood pressure, which are so important for prevention techniques, derives from epidemiological studies. Similarly, population studies have shown that prolonged cigarette smoking from early adult life triples age-specific mortality rates, but cessation at the age of 50 reduces the danger by half, and cessation at the age of 30 eliminates the danger almost completely. . . .

2. Studies on Patients

The main source of medical knowledge has always been the direct study of human disease by closely monitoring human patients. For example, cardiologist Dean Ornish has demonstrated that a low-fat vegetarian diet, regular exercise, smoking cessation and stress management can reverse heart disease. Similarly, Caldwell Esselstyn has shown that lowering cholesterol levels with plant-based diets and medicines as needed arrests and often reverses heart disease. Henry Heimlich has relied exclusively on human clinical investigation to develop techniques and operations that have saved thousands of lives, including the Heimlich maneuver for choking and drowning victims, the Heimlich operation to replace the esophagus (throat tube), and the Heimlich chest drainage valve. . . .

3. Autopsies and Biopsies

The autopsy rate in the United States and Europe has been falling steadily, much to the dismay of clinical investigators who recognize the value of this traditional research tool. Autopsies have been crucial to our current understanding of many diseases, e.g. heart disease, appendicitis, diabetes and Alzheimer's disease. Although the usefulness of autopsies is generally limited to the disease's lethal stage, biopsies can provide information about other disease stages. Diagnostic needle and endoscopic biopsies often permit safe procurement of human tissues from living patients. . . . Small skin biopsies (with intact capillaries) can be used as a tool before or during clinical trials of new drugs and could have revealed the cardiovascular risks of Vioxx, for example, before it was marketed.

4. Post-Marketing Surveillance

Thanks to advances in computer techniques, it is now possible to keep detailed and comprehensive records of drug side effects. A central database with such information, derived from post-marketing surveillance, enables rapid identification of dangerous drugs. Such a data system would also increase the likelihood that unexpected beneficial side effects of drugs would be recognized. Indeed, the anti-cancer properties of such medications as prednisone, nitrogen mustard and actinomycin D; chlorpromazine's tranquilizing effect; and the mood-elevating effect of MAO-inhibitors and tricyclic antidepressants were all discovered through clinical observation of side effects. . . .

Why Animal Experimentation Persists

If animal experimentation is so flawed, why does it persist? There are several likely explanations.

1. **For the chemical and pharmaceutical industries, animal experiments provide an important legal sanctu-**

ary. In cases of death or disability caused by chemical products or adverse drug reactions, the responsible companies claim due diligence by pointing out that they performed the legally prescribed "safety tests" on animals and are therefore not accountable. As a result, the victims or their families most often come away empty-handed after suing for damages.

2. **Animal experimentation is easily published.** In the "publish or perish" world of academic science, it requires little originality or insight to take an already well-defined animal model, change a variable or the species being used, and obtain "new" and "interesting" findings within a short period of time. In contrast, clinical research, while directly applicable to humans, is more difficult, expensive and time-consuming. . . .

3. **Animal experimentation is self-perpetuating.** Scientists' salaries and professional status are often tied to grants, and a critical element of success in grant applications is proof of prior experience and expertise. Researchers trained in animal experimentation techniques find it difficult or inconvenient to adopt new methods such as tissue cultures.

4. **Animal experimentation is lucrative.** Its traditionally respected place in modern medicine results in secure financial support, which is often an integral component of a university's budget. Many medical centers receive several hundred million dollars annually in direct grants for animal research, and an average of over 40% more for overhead costs that are supposedly related to that research. Since many medical centers faced with declining clinical revenues depend on this financial windfall for much of their administrative costs, construction and building maintenance, they perpetuate animal experimentation by praising it in the media and to legislators.

5. **Animal experimentation appears more "scientific" than clinical research**. Researchers often assert that laboratory experiments are "controlled" because they can change one variable at a time. This control, however, is illusory. Any animal model differs in myriad ways from human physiology and pathology. In addition, the laboratory setting itself creates confounding variables—for example, stress and undesired or unrecognized pathology in the animals. Such variables can have system-wide effects, skew experimental results, and undermine extrapolation of findings to humans.

6. **The morality of animal experimentation is rarely questioned by researchers, who generally choose to defend the practice dogmatically, rather than confront the obvious moral issues it raises**. Animal experimenters' language betrays their efforts to avoid morality. For example, they "sacrifice" animals rather than kill them, and they may note animal "distress", but they rarely acknowledge pain or other suffering. Young scientists quickly learn to adopt such a mind-set from their superiors, as sociologist Arnold Arluke explains. "One message—almost a warning—that newcomers got was that it was controversial or risky to admit to having ethical concerns, because to do so was tantamount to admitting that there really was something morally wrong with animal experimentation, thereby giving 'ammunition to the enemy.'" Physician E. J. Moore also observes: "Sadly, young doctors must say nothing, at least in public, about the abuse or laboratory animals, for fear of jeopardizing their career prospects."

Evidence indicates that many animal experimenters fail to acknowledge—or even perceive—animal pain and suffering. For example, sociologist Mary Phillips observed animal experimenters kill rats in acute toxicity tests, induce cancer in rodents, subject animals to major surgery with no postoperative analgesia, and perform numerous other painful procedures without administering anesthesia or analgesia to the animals. Nevertheless, in their annual reports to the U.S. Department of Agriculture (USDA), none of the researchers acknowledged that any animals had experienced unrelieved pain or distress. Phillips reported: "Over and over, researchers assured me that in their laboratories, animals were never hurt ... 'Pain' meant the acute pain of surgery on conscious animals, and almost nothing else ... [When I asked] about psychological or emotional suffering, many researchers were at a loss to answer." ...

The value of animal experimentation has been grossly exaggerated by those with a vested economic interest in its preservation.

The tens of millions of animals used and killed each year in American laboratories generally suffer enormously, often from fear and physical pain, and nearly always from the deprivation inflicted by their confinement which denies their most basic psychological and physical needs.

The value of animal experimentation has been grossly exaggerated by those with a vested economic interest in its preservation. Because animal experimentation focuses on artificially created pathology, involves confounding variables, and is undermined by differences between human and nonhuman anatomy, physiology and pathology, it is an inherently unsound method to investigate human disease processes. The billions of dollars invested annually in animal experimentation would be put to much more efficient, effective and humane use if redirected to clinical and epidemiological research and public health programs.

Superior Research Methods Make Animal Testing Unjustified

Alistair Currie

Alistair Currie is senior research and campaigns coordinator for the United Kingdom affiliate of People for the Ethical Treatment of Animals (PETA), a well-known animal rights organization.

New figures showing that the number of animals used in laboratories in the EU [European Union] is on the rise are cause for alarm—and not just because of the enormous amount of suffering involved. Continuing to rely upon animal experiments when we have superior research methods available is simply bad public policy.

According to the figures, the number of animals used in experiments increased by 3.2% between 2002 and 2005, even when the additional experiments of the 10 new member states are excluded. More than 12 million animals were used overall, with the UK [United Kingdom] placing second only to France in numbers used. Britain's own official figures show a consistent trend upwards, and the highest figures since 1992.

Shockingly, despite public concern and claims of tight legislation, the number of animals used in cosmetics tests increased 50%. If even this most universally reviled use of animals is uncontrolled by legislation and the sanction of public disapproval, it is abundantly clear that real action is required. (Cosmetics testing on animals is being gradually ended by the EU's Cosmetics Directive but the law governing animal experiments lacks the teeth to do anything about it.)

Numerically, cosmetics tests are a tiny part of the picture, but the failure of existing measures to curb them is a telling symptom of animal experimentation as a whole. Take recent "supermice" stories—hyped examples of genetic manipulation that are manna from heaven for headline writers but classic examples of speculative research, indulging scientific curiosity justified by spurious claims of long-term human benefit. Animal suffering is perpetually justified by the cure round the corner, but decades of animal research on AIDS vaccines, strokes, Alzheimer's and multiple sclerosis have failed to deliver.

A series of recent studies has highlighted the poor predictability of animal tests. In 2004 a *British Medical Journal* study concluded that scientific claims on behalf of animal experimentation were largely anecdotal, while one in 2006 revealed that animal experiments predicted human outcomes only in a third of cases studied. Most damningly, US Food and Drug Administration figures show that 92% of drugs which pass animal trials are found to be unsafe or ineffective in human trials and never reach the market.

In safety testing, PETA [People for the Ethical Treatment of Animals] reviewed more than 500 rodent cancer studies to assess their scientific validity and round that critical public health and worker protection measures were delayed for many years because of misplaced trust in animal tests, which could not easily replicate cancerous effects which had already been documented in humans. About one in every seven rodent cancer studies is judged to be inadequate or to have produced ambiguous results, which are therefore disregarded by health authorities.

The permissive approach towards animal experiments must end.

The failings of tests such as these are well known in the scientific and regulatory communities but efforts by scientists, companies and official bodies to replace them are often stymied by inertia, bureaucracy and almost criminal apathy. New non-animal toxicity tests must, rightly, be validated to ensure they are reliable and accurate—but that process can take decades and the animal tests themselves have never been scientifically validated. In that process, non-animal techniques are compared with animal tests: the result can be that new techniques which are better at predicting human effects fail to match the inaccurate results of the animal tests and so are judged deficient. The tortuous process of gaining acceptance for non-animal methods is a cross between [the surrealist writings of Franz] Kafka and [Joseph Heller's novel] *Catch-22*.

Animal Research Must End

The permissive approach towards animal experiments must end. . . . While PETA advocates an immediate end to all animal experiments and will continue to call for a complete ban, we're realists. Measures such as allowing public access to information regarding animal experiments, preventing duplication of tests and, critically, ensuring genuine assessment of studies' possible benefits relative to the suffering involved, could make a world of difference to the animals infected, poisoned, genetically manipulated and surgically mutilated in EU labs every year.

At the very least, we must stop casually giving the green light to the bottomless pit of questionable animal tests which delay needed protections, mislead researchers, waste precious resources, and inflict utterly unacceptable suffering on animals.

Using Animals for Medical Testing May Be Wrong for Scientific Rather than Ethical Reasons

Arthur Allen

Arthur Allen is a journalist based in Washington, D.C.

Every year, in the name of medical progress, scientists breed and nurture hundreds of millions of mice, rats, and other subordinate mammals. Then they expose the critters to substances that could become the next Zocors, Prozacs, and Avastins [all best-selling drugs]. Since the alternative is to experiment on people, most everyone other than hardcore animal lovers accepts animal testing. Periodically, however, a spectacular failure raises new questions about the enterprise—not for ethical reasons, but scientific ones.

In March, London clinicians injected six volunteers with tiny doses of TGN1412, an experimental therapy for rheumatoid arthritis and multiple sclerosis that had previously been given, with no obvious ill effects, to mice, rats, rabbits, and monkeys. Within minutes, the human test subjects were writhing on the floor in agony. The compound was designed to dampen the immune response but it had supercharged theirs, unleashing a cascade of chemicals that sent all six to the hospital. Several of the men suffered permanent organ damage, and one man's head swelled up so horribly that British tabloids refer to the case as the "elephant man trial."

Animal rights activists in Britain pounced, declaring the uselessness of animal experimentation in the development of human drugs. A group called Uncaged declared that it was immoral "to subject animals to painful, distressing and lethal experiments when the results are not applicable to humans." This is fundamentally dishonest, of course—there would be no medical advance without animal experimentation. Examples range from Frederick Banting and Charles Best's diabetic dogs, which proved the existence of insulin in the 1920s, to the mice who confirmed the value of anti-angiogenesis drugs, which block the growth of blood vessels that feed tumors. Still, it is true that animal tests, even on multiple species, do not always predict the toxicity of pharmaceuticals or industrial chemicals in humans. This doesn't make animal testing any less crucial to the development and testing of drugs. But in an era in which drug development is growing increasingly sophisticated, it may point to the need for new designs in animal testing.

Over the years, toxicologists have developed rules of thumb for which animals will best model the toxic symptoms they expect in man. An early example was the canary in the coal mine. As the Bureau of Mines' George A. Burrell noted in 1912, in the presence of excess carbon monoxide, "a bird sways noticeably on its perch before falling, and its fall is a better indication of danger than is the squatting, extended posture that some poisoned mice assume." Dogs, it turns out—usually beagles, in particular—are man's best test animal, in that the same compounds frequently sicken dogs and their masters (though dogs tend to vomit more than we do).

"There is no reliable way of predicting what type of toxicity will develop in different species to the same compound."

But just how often do animal tests predict side effects in humans? Surprisingly, although it is central to the legitimacy of animal testing, only a dozen or so scholars over the past 30 years have explored this question. The results, such as they are, have been somewhat discouraging. One of the scientists, Ralph Heywood, stated in 1989 that "there is no reliable way of predicting what type of toxicity will develop in different species to the same compound." The concordance between man and animal toxicity tests, he said, assessing three decades of studies on the subject, was somewhere below 25 percent. "Toxicology," concluded Heywood, "is a science without a scientific underpinning."

In 1999, the Health and Environmental Sciences Institute, a Washington, D.C.-based group that brings together business, academic, and government experts to assess risks in public health, began a thorough examination. Working with confidential data provided by 12 pharmaceutical companies on 150 compounds that had produced a variety of toxic effects in people, an institute-hosted workshop found that only 43 percent of the drugs produced similar problems in rodents, and 63 percent did so in nonrodents. These are not reassuring numbers. (Though they would look better if the institute's review had included the 90 percent of drug candidates that are screened out by animal toxicity, and thus never even tested on humans.)

Industry, academic, and government scientists agree that science is in need of better animal models for testing drug safety. "Put simply, the inability to predict the human toxicity of drugs is what's breaking the promise of genomics to drug development," says Paul Watkins, a North Carolina physician who is advising the institute. The high-tech biology era has seen the discovery of thousands of new targets for pharmaceuticals, but the number of drug failures remains as high as ever. It's painful for the drug industry when $500 million goes toward developing a drug that then must be scrapped because of side effects that only surface in human trials. And it's bad for the public as well when a product like Rezulin, Warner-

Lambert's diabetes drug, is withdrawn from the market for causing liver disease and deaths after 800,000 patients have taken it.

It's painful for the drug industry when . . . a drug . . . must be scrapped because of side effects that only surface in human trials.

An equal source of human suffering may be the dozens of promising drugs that get shelved when they cause problems in animals that may not be relevant for humans. Studies of the comparative biology of humans and animals have established that some problems in animals aren't worrisome for humans. For example, during preclinical, high-dosage tests of Viagra, the drug constipated mice, swelled rat livers, and gave beagle dogs "beagle pain syndrome," which included arching of the back and stiffness—in the neck. Pfizer's scientists determined, correctly, that these side effects had no relevance to humans.

A Lack of Reliable Test Animals

Since drugs often fail by causing side effects in small groups of vulnerable people who take them (think Vioxx), scientists try to breed and use rodents with special problems—the "hypertensive rat"—to eliminate drugs that will hurt special medical populations. But such methods don't stop government regulators from insisting on tried-and-true animal-testing schemes, because doing the same experiment on each new drug means the result can be measured against a historical record. Drug companies have grown restive under certain requirements, such as the two-year rat test for carcinogenicity, which, it is generally agreed, isn't reliable. Edward Calabrese, a University of Massachusetts toxicologist, once wrote that "it seems almost incredible that the rat is the model so heavily relied upon when predicting human responses to toxic carcinogenic agents" given the "profound differences between the values of the human and the rat" in many bodily processes.

The hope has been that thousands of new lines of transgenic mice—with genes knocked out, inserted, or imported from the human genome—will prove the perfect test animals. But that's not likely. Tinkering with a few genes doesn't make them perfect stand-ins for people. In 2003, for example, Elan Pharmaceuticals had to stop trials of an Alzheimer's vaccine that had cured the disease in "Alzheimer's mice," after the substance caused brain inflammation in human test subjects.

And then there's the monoclonal antibody TGN1412, an artificial antibody designed to bind to certain T-cell receptors, thereby cutting off autoimmune attacks. Instead of dousing the immune response, TGN1412 seems to have bound to cells in a way that unleashed a chemical chain reaction. Animal tests are particularly tricky for monoclonal antibodies—a hot area of development for cancer and autoimmune disease—because these drugs target very complex, specific human proteins. According to a recent FDA-authored review article, only chimpanzees and humans provide realistic models for testing many monoclonal antibodies. And even our fellow primates have divergent immune systems. They can be infected with HIV-like viruses, for example, without getting sick. Plus, the endangered chimps are not the ideal test animals. Different as they are, they seem too much like us to be guinea pigs.

CHAPTER 4

Should It Be Allowed for Animals to Be Used for Entertainment?

Chapter Preface

Horse racing, a multibillion-dollar industry popular with many people, especially those who like to bet on races, is viewed by animal advocates as cruel and unfair to the racehorses themselves.

Advocates say most horses bred for racing are forced to train or race before their skeletons are mature enough to handle the pressures of running on a hard racetrack at high speeds. They typically are purchased (sometimes for hundreds of thousands of dollars) by large syndicates rather than individuals, and owners want to see a quick return on their money. They are then handled by numerous trainers, handlers, veterinarians, and jockeys, preventing them from developing a close relationship with any one person. Most racehorses also are trucked, flown, or otherwise shipped to thousands of racetracks throughout the country or world, and are constantly prepared to run as fast as they possibly can, race after race, throughout their lives.

According to animal activists, another major problem with horse racing is that many racehorses are given drugs to help them run faster or to keep them racing when they are injured or in pain. Some drugs are legal, but many are illegal under racing rules. The temptation to use drugs on horses, experts say, is high because of the large amounts of money that are involved in racing and related gambling operations.

The pressure of this strenuous and stressful racing life results in numerous injuries to the animals. According to a factsheet prepared by People for the Ethical Treatment of Animals (PETA), studies have shown that one horse in every twenty-two races suffers an injury that prevents it from finishing a race, and approximately eight hundred thoroughbreds die each year in North America because of injuries. Injuries tend to be strained tendons or hairline fractures that are difficult for veterinarians to diagnose, and if a horse runs with these types of injuries, it could easily break a leg. Broken legs are often a death sentence for horses, because of the cost and difficulty of getting such large animals to wear casts or live in slings until their bodies can heal. Because this type of injury usually means the horse can no longer race, and the cost of putting a horse out to pasture for the rest of its life is substantial, more often than not, horses with serious injuries are euthanized by owners.

Those racehorses that survive the brutal demands of racing typically end their lives in slaughterhouses. In the United States, tens of thousands of horses are slaughtered every year and the meat exported to countries where people eat horsemeat. A significant number of these horses are former racehorses. And since there are only two horse slaughterhouses in the country, the horses first have to endure a days-long ride in cramped trailers, sometimes with no food or water, to get to the place where they will die. According to PETA, this often results in injuries to the animals. The final slaughter is accomplished by cutting the horses' throats; this is supposed to be preceded by a shot to the head with a pneumatic gun or some similar method to render them oblivious to pain. Animal advocates claim, however, that horses often become frightened and flail about, making the euthanasia difficult and giving the horses a very traumatic death.

Concern about the plight of racehorses has led to the establishment of numerous rescue organizations throughout the country. These organizations try to save racehorses from the slaughterhouses, rehabilitate them for use in pleasure riding, and adopt them out to individuals who will love and care for them. One such organization, for example, is Tranquility Farm in Tehachapi, California. The group accepts donations of thoroughbred horses from the racetrack and tries to give each horse the chance to find an adoptive home. If a horse is not readily adoptable, the group provides comfortable retirement whenever possible, prioritizing those horses that have been significant competitors or producers in racing. The farm encourages owners of the racehorses to contribute funds to help defray the costs of rehabilitation and retraining, but no horse is denied acceptance based on an owner's failure to make a financial contribution. For some lucky racehorses, therefore, there is a bright ending to their racing career.

Horseracing is only one of the ways that humans use animals for entertainment or recreational purposes. Animals also are asked to perform for humans in rodeos, circuses, and marine parks; wild animals are captured and confined in zoos for human inspection; and animals are killed for pleasure by those who hunt and fish. The various pros and cons of using animals to entertain or pleasure humans are the subject of the viewpoints in this chapter.

Sportfishing Does Not Hurt Fish

Dave Lear

Dave Lear is a professional fishing guide in Florida and the former executive director of The Billfish Foundation, a nonprofit organization dedicated to conserving and enhancing billfish populations around the world.

They're back. People for the Ethical Treatment of Animals (PETA) is launching another all-out assault on sportfishing. The group's ultimate goal is to ban the sport entirely. To reach that goal this time around, PETA is trying to portray fish as intelligent, sensitive creatures that feel pain when they are hooked or yanked from the water. "No one would ever put a hook through a dog's or a cat's mouth," says Bruce Friedrich, the organization's director of vegan outreach. "Once people start to understand that fish, although they come in different packaging, are just as intelligent, they'll stop eating them."

As evidence, PETA cites a couple of European studies, including one by Edinburgh's Roslin Institute (the same folks who cloned Dolly the sheep) that recorded fish reactions to mechanical, thermal and chemical stimulation. This research discovered numerous receptors on the heads of trout that responded to the stimuli. But whether that proves fish feel pain or not is still subject to debate.

"A fish brain does not have the cerebral cortex that mammals and more advanced critters do," says Dr. Russell Nelson, a Florida-based fisheries scientist and sportfisherman. "And those are the areas of the brain where pain stimuli are processed. Certainly, fish feel discomfort when they are handled or pulled on a line, but they don't react to pain the way that people or dogs do."

I'm definitely one of those people who believes that fish don't feel pain. I've caught, tagged and released fish only to have the same one hook up again minutes later. I've watched dozens of sailfish throw up their stomachs after a hook-set, just as they do naturally after swallowing a bait-fish and getting stabbed by fin bones. Ever had a fish swim on contentedly after it is hooked? I often have the impression that once it finally feels the pull of the line, it's screaming adios, but only in a quest for freedom, not because it hurts.

Catch-and-Release Fishing

PETA's latest campaign is called the Fish Empathy Project, and it doesn't cut anglers any slack, even those who practice catch-and-release fishing. The word *sport* earns quotation marks on the organization's Web site. And it's not only the "catch" part of catch-and-release that's deemed objectionable. High release mortality is cited as yet another aspect of fishing's pervasive cruelty, despite the fact that, depending on the species and the way a fish is caught, release mortality can be negligible—as low as zero, according to some billfish studies.

> *With modern tackle and techniques, and the acceptance of catch-and-release, [sportfishing has] gone from blood sport towards an opportunity to be on the water and appreciate the marine life.*

In the sport's fledgling years, when bragging rights meant throwing every boated fish on the dock, PETA's Fish Empathy Project might have had more credibility. But those times are long gone, thank goodness. "Sportfishing certainly started out as a blood sport," Nelson says. "But it has now evolved well beyond that. With modern tackle and techniques, and the acceptance of catch-and-release, we've gone from blood sport towards an opportunity to be on the water and appreciate the marine life below the surface."

Sorry, PETA. Buy all the billboard and magazine ads you want, and keep on boycotting seafood restaurants if you have to. I'll still be out there fishing, even if my boat does get a little bloody on occasion.

Is Bear Hunting Necessary to Protect Both Bears and Humans?

Sara B. Miller

It has been described as a battle between North and South, between urban and rural, between Old Maine and New Maine.

At issue? A bear referendum, which would outlaw hunting of Maine's black bears with the help of stale jelly doughnuts and other "bait," leg-hold traps, or hound dogs. . . .

Supporters say that luring bears with bait while hunters wait in place, trapping them, or employing dogs to chase the animals up trees is cruel and against a "fair chase" standard. Opponents, including the governor, claim the bear population will flourish if the initiative passes and that significant money is at stake.

Support breaks down geographically, with the forested north pitted against the more populated south. "It cuts very strongly north to south," says Christian Potholm, a pollster and professor of government at Bowdoin College in Brunswick, Me. Yet despite common stereotypes that hunters tend to be gun-toting Republicans and animal rights groups Democrats, the question does not break down by party affiliation. "It is quite nonpartisan," Mr. Potholm says.

The conflict between bear and human has surfaced in other states. The legality of bear baiting in Alaska is being questioned . . . too. Bear hunting is currently allowed in 28 states. Eleven allow baiting, while 17 permit hunting with hounds. Maine has the largest bear population east of the

Mississippi River, with 23,000. Some 4,000 are killed by hunters each year, the far majority with bait. It is the only state to allow trapping.

Bears can self-regulate, and . . . a ban would not necessarily diminish the number of out-of-state hunters—who make up about half of the state's bear hunters.

On a crisp fall day, Bill Randall places a tree limb in a trap, whose teethed jaws quickly snarl it. Whack. It slams shut. Mr. Randall, a former hunter who used to trap bears, is a lead proponent of doing away with bear trapping, baiting, and hounding. It was a gradual change of heart. "It is a learning curve, an appreciation of wildlife that comes with aging and education," he says.

The Benefits and Downfalls of Bear Control

Like other referendum supporters, Randall has drawn the ire of the hunting community. "It would be so hard to hunt bears without the use of bait that the number of kills would drop," says Tim Barry, a hunting guide in Kingfield, Me. And that would surely cause a spike in nuisance calls, now about 300 a year, he says, and could mean bears in backyards and near schools.

Whether bear management will spiral out of control and how much money is at stake if the referendum passes is contentious. Opponents estimate $62 million would be lost in food, hotel, licensing, and other expenses related to hunting. Supporters claim the number is much smaller. They also say bears can self-regulate, and that a ban would not necessarily diminish the number of out-of-state hunters—who make up about half of the state's bear hunters.

Beyond geography, the ballot initiative has turned into a class struggle too—as the south has been painted as a place where "cruel yuppies" don't understand or care about the livelihood of the rural north, says Potholm.

Indeed, many suburbanites don't understand a Maine tradition, says Barry. Dogs have been chasing bears in Maine's woods since the colonial era. Besides, he says, it's tough work despite the assertion that baiting, hounding, and trapping are short cuts for fast cash.

You could never end hunting in Maine . . . not in a million years.

Randall disagrees. And he says opponents are playing on state pride to attract followers, warning residents not to let New Maine tell real Mainers what to do. He says it is an unnecessary tactic, that the referendum targets methods of hunting, not hunting itself. "You could never end hunting in Maine," says Randall, "not in a million years."

Circus Animals Are Well Treated

James Randerson

James Randerson is a science correspondent for the Guardian, *a British newspaper.*

Sinbad and Zebadee [two circus zebras] will be pounding the sawdust under their big top for a while longer thanks to a [British] government-backed report which concluded there was no evidence that circus animals were kept in worse conditions than animals in other captive environments. The result will delight the four British circuses out of 27 that still use animals in their acts—including Circus Mondao, which keeps the two performing zebras. But ministers at the Department for Environment, Food and Rural Affairs are left with an awkward decision on whether to ban wild animals in circuses after the report they commissioned into the science of animal welfare gave little to go on. Animal circuses are much less common in Britain than in Europe. Although it is possible to watch acts including crocodiles, lions, snakes and even a kangaroo, the report estimates just 47 animals work regularly in circus rings in [Britain].

The circus community argues that animal shows are an important part of our cultural heritage, that the animals only perform natural behaviours and are kept to the best possible welfare standards.

Animal rights organisations argue that subjecting animals to training and transport between venues for entertainment is unethical. They are furious the working group which produced the report was given a restricted remit to look only at transportation and housing needs of non-domesticated species and not training.

On this question the report concludes there is not enough good scientific evidence to make the case either way. "For the status quo to be changed the balance of evidence would have to present a convincing and coherent argument for change," the working group's academic panel of six animal welfare experts wrote. "Such an argument, based on a sound scientific basis, has not been made. . . . There appears to be little evidence to demonstrate that the welfare of animals kept in travelling circuses is any better or worse than that of animals kept in other captive environments."

You can go to a county show and see people doing dog agility, but when you see people doing dog agility in a circus it all of a sudden becomes wrong.

Animal rights campaigners were dismayed at the judgment. "We didn't need a report telling us something that we already knew, which is the lack of peer reviewed studies on the treatment of circus animals," said a spokeswoman for the RSPCA [Royal Society for the Prevention of Cruelty to Animals]. She said that although there were few studies on exotic species, studies of the transportation of other species such as farm animals could be applied.

Those on the industry side say the report negates what they regard as a prolonged campaign of smears linking circuses with cruelty. "The animal rights people have made that word *circus* so dirty," said Petra Jackson, ringmistress at Circus Mondao. "People have got to open their eyes and see what circus is about now and not what it was about 30 years ago. I really do think it is snobbery. You can go to a county show and see people doing dog agility, but when you see people doing dog agility in a circus it all of a sudden becomes wrong."

Chris Barltropp of the union Equity was chairman of the industry sub-committee which contributed to the report. "It does seem that the circus community has been vindicated by this report. At last we have reached a point where we can set aside the name calling which has been going on for years from the animal rights organisations," he said.

An Uncertain Future for Circuses

The report leaves [British government] ministers in a tricky position. Many MPs [members of Parliament] and peers are in favour of a ban. In March 2006, [MP and minister of state in the Department of Health] Ben Bradshaw ... said in Parliament: "I sympathise with the view that performances by some wild animals in travelling circuses are not compatible with meeting welfare needs." He said the government wanted to introduce regulations under the Animal Welfare Act rather than through primary legislation, but the author of the current report believes that will not be possible. Mike Radford, an expert on the legal aspects of animal welfare at Aberdeen University, said: "[Ministers] gave commitments in Parliament that a ban would be based on scientific evidence and as yet there isn't any." Responding to the report, the environment secretary, Hilary Benn, said: "The government will now want to hear reactions ... and consider its position."

An Ipsos Mori opinion poll in October 2005 for Animal Defenders International found that 80% of people agree that the use of wild animals in circuses should be banned—65% thought that all performing animals should be banned.

Traditional Rodeos Should Be Allowed to Continue

Lorne Gunter

Lorne Gunter is a Canadian journalist who blogs at the Comment section of the National Post, *a Canadian newspaper.*

The Cloverdale Rodeo and Country Fair in Surrey, B.C. [British Columbia] bills itself as "a celebration of western lifestyle." Well, no longer. After a calf had to be euthanized . . . following the roping competition, organizers of the 119-year-old event capitulated to pressure from animal rights groups (and its own increasingly urbanized, politically correct board) by banning calf-roping, team roping, steer wrestling and wild cow milking. Cloverdale's directors hailed their decision as "progressive" and "with the times." But in reality, it is further evidence that as Canadian society moves away from its rural roots, we are falsely romanticizing and anthropomorphizing animals.

Protecting Rodeo Livestock

We wish we could blame the rodeo's decision entirely on animal rights activists, some of whom tried to disrupt [a recent] event by forcing their way onto the rodeo infield to block competition. But the truth is, rodeo's sanctioning bodies have caused some of their sport's own problems. Just as some overly concerned pet lovers have started referring to their pets by the politically correct term "non-human companions," rodeo organizations have—with an eye to deflecting criticism—taken to calling rodeo stock "animal athletes." On the surface, this may seem to give the bulls, horses, steers and calves used in

Lorne Gunter, "Circle the Wagons: Lorne Gunter on the Animal-Rights Threat to Canadian Rodeos," *National Post*, May 23, 2007. Reproduced by permission. http://network.nationalpost.com/np/blogs/fullcomment/archive/2007/05/23/circle-the-wagons-lorne-gunter-on-the-animal-rights-threat-to-canadian-rodeos.aspx.

rodeo a higher level of respect. But by reinforcing the notion that the livestock are active participants with a stake in the competition, this terminology feeds rodeo's opponents' argument that the animals understand what is going on at rodeos and feel distress from it.

All major rodeo associations and professional rodeo-competitors organizations have codes of conduct mandating the humane treatment of livestock.

Cowboys and stock contractors who supply animals to rodeos already do their utmost to protect the livestock. Most major rodeos feature an animal protection society officer whose job it is to ensure no animal is mistreated. As people who handle animals for a living, too, most riders, ropers and contractors understand better than those who would shut them down what the stock can and cannot tolerate without injury or duress. It benefits neither the competitors nor the contractors when animals are injured. All major rodeo associations and professional rodeo-competitors organizations have codes of conduct mandating the humane treatment of livestock. There are even Internet sites on which fans follow the performances of the best bulls and broncs, whose names and attributes are known to hardcore rodeo watchers, and chat rooms in which fans debate what can and should be done to protect rodeo animals.

The End of Rodeos

Eventually, the rodeo as we know it may become endangered in Canada: Marcie Moriarty, B.C. SPCA [Society for the Prevention of Cruelty to Animals] general manager of cruelty investigations, said eliminating these four events was merely "a step in the right direction" for Cloverdale. Having scored this victory, urban types will sense an opening, and press for the elimination of any competition involving animals from not only Cloverdale but all rodeos.

Far fewer Canadians make their living off the land than a century ago, when rodeos first became common at summer fairs. But the sport remains as popular as ever. More of us, for instance, attend a rodeo each year than attend a professional hockey game. The sport is a straightforward contest between man and animal, and a worthwhile connection to our past. It would be a shame if other rodeos encouraged those who would water down, or even eliminate, this wonderful tradition by following Cloverdale's timid example.

Bullfighting Should Be Banned

Caroline Lucas

Caroline Lucas is an English politician. She is currently a Member of the European Parliament (MEP) for the South East England region and the female principal speaker of the Green Party of England and Wales. She is one of two Green MEPs from the United Kingdom.

In the European Parliament [in early June 2008], I chaired an open seminar on the future of bullfighting in the EU. Although its organisers originate from varying backgrounds—European animal welfare, veterinary science and economics—they all agree on one thing: bullfighting has to go.

Despite a considerable number of states having banned the practice of bullfighting by law—Argentina, Canada, Cuba, Denmark, Germany, Italy, the Netherlands, New Zealand and the United Kingdom among them—it still takes place in nine countries around the world. This is nine countries too many. Yet it is encouraging to find that even where bullfighting is legal, certain regions have begun to phase it out, such as the Canary Islands in Spain, and most of France.

Public appetite for this cruel blood sport has long been on the wane, but that doesn't stop the Spanish government from heavily subsidising the declining industry. It has been estimated that over 550 million euros of taxpayer money is allocated to the pro-bullfighting industry per year, even though Spanish broadcaster RTVE stopped live coverage of bullfights in August 2007 and recent Gallup polls showed that the majority of Spaniards either disliked bullfighting or had no interest in it. Worse still, the EU subsidises it. According to recent reports, breeders of fighting bulls receive 220 Euros per bull per year from the EU, on top of national subsidies. Yet the EU is supposed to be a community of values—one of which is a high level of animal protection.

Bullfighting Is a Cruel, Unequal Game

The pro bullfighting lobby puts forward a number of claims for the preservation of the 'sport', which need be addressed. First though, it is worth considering the reality of a typical Spanish-style bullfight. The 'show' begins when the bull enters the arena and is provoked into charging several times, before being approached by picadores, men on blindfolded horses, who drive lances into its back and neck muscles. The subsequent loss of blood impairs the bull's ability to lift its head, and when the banderilleros arrive on foot, the bull can expect further pain from the banderillas, spiked sticks in bright colours, being stabbed into its back.

Now weak and disorientated, the bull is encouraged by the banderilleros to run in dizzying circles before finally, the matador appears and, after a few forced charges, tries to kill the bull with his sword. If he misses, he stabs the submissive animal on the back of the neck until it is paralysed. The idea is to cut the animal's spinal cord, but if the matador botches the job, the bull may be fully conscious while its ears or tail are removed as trophies. On many occasions, the bull remains alive until it is dragged out of the arena to be slaughtered.

Thousands of bulls are maimed and killed in such a way every year. Spain puts the official number of bulls killed in official bullfights in permanent bullrings in 2006 at 11,458, but when you take into account the bullfights in mobile bullrings and the bulls killed during training and other bullfighting events, the figure is more likely to reach at least 40,000 in Europe as a whole, and about 250,000 internationally.

A continuation of the 'sport' has been justified on the grounds of national cultural heritage, some on ecological grounds, while others believe that it plays an important part

in a country's economy. Such claims have been effectively re-
futed by animal welfare organisations, as well as by politicians
and economists from across the political spectrum. Even
Queen Sofia of Spain has expressed her dislike for the
'tradition'.

Some have defended bullfighting as a national tradition,
seeking to preserve it as a piece of cultural heritage without
which their country's identity would suffer. Nevertheless, many
others have opposed it, recognising bullfighting for what it really is—a cruel blood sport causing unnecessary suffering to
the animal.

---

*There is no place in the 21st century for a 'sport' which
relies on animal cruelty for 'entertainment.'*

Even if you believe that bullfighting is a tradition or culture, the fact that it dates back to prehistoric times and that
artists have revered it can never really justify serious cruelty to
animals. Cruelty is cruelty no matter where in the world it
happens. Human societies and cultures have changed over
many thousands of years, as has what traditions are deemed
acceptable. Our understanding of animals has improved a
great deal in recent times. There is no place in the 21st century for a 'sport' which relies on animal cruelty for
'entertainment'.

The ecological argument is also tenuous. The bullfighting
industry points out that many fighting bulls are bred in semi-
preserved areas of land called dehesas, home to several protected species and cared for as areas of outstanding natural
beauty. The industry claims that these areas will disappear if
bullfighting is abolished, because their business prevents the
dehesas being developed for other purposes.

But the breeding of fighting bulls is not the sole purpose
and function of this land, plus local authorities have never
identified the bulls' removal as a threat to populations of pro-

tected species. The owners of the dehesas can choose to use their land in a variety of ways regardless of whether or not they keep bulls, and those that do keep bulls should be compensated for loss of activity. It is the job of local authorities to ensure that such land and wildlife is protected, and the necessary laws are already in place. Furthermore, the Foro Encinal, an alliance of twenty organisations whose role is to protect the dehesas, has never identified the breeding of fighting bulls as beneficial to the land's ecological balance.

A Vital Tourist Industry?

Economic concerns focus on bullfighting as a vital part of the tourist industry in Spain; as a generator of money and as an employer of people. Yet, tourists will visit Spain regardless of whether or not bullfighting exists, and as people become more ethically aware on their travels, tourist attendance at the shows looks set to fall even further. Indeed, a ComRes poll commissioned in April 2007 found that 89% of the British public would not visit a bullfight when on a holiday.

Statistics show clearly that the opposition to bullfighting is growing throughout Europe, and that it is no longer deemed acceptable for the EU or for national governments to subsidize an activity which relies on animal abuse to make money.

Like most industries, the profits from bullfighting end up in the hands of a very small number of people in a bullfighting elite. Even more importantly, the subsidies that prop up this declining industry take money away from serious social problems such as access to public health, education, infrastructures, the elderly, public safety, social housing and environmental policies.

In Spain, the country perhaps most associated with the bullfighting tradition, a 2006 Gallup poll showed that 72.10

per cent of Spaniards were not interested at all in bullfighting and just 7.40 per cent were very interested; in Catalonia more than 80 per cent showed no interest at all.

Undemocratic Use of Funds

Such statistics show clearly that the opposition to bullfighting is growing throughout Europe, and that it is no longer deemed acceptable for the EU or for national governments to subsidise an activity which relies on animal abuse to make money. It seems undemocratic at best to use cash from the public coffers to prop up an unpopular blood sport, at the expense of crucial public services.

It is our responsibility to ensure that adequate protection is provided for animals in our care to prevent unnecessary suffering. I call on the European Parliament to reconsider the financial assistance given to the breeders of fighting bulls, so that the efforts to ban the 'sport' altogether can gather pace. The longer that bull fighting persists, the longer our standards of animal welfare will fall short of the mark.

Sport Hunting Should Be Banned

Delaware Action for Animals

Delaware Action for Animals is an organization that works to end animal exploitation and protect and enhance the lives of all animals living in the state of Delaware.

There once was a time when most Americans needed to hunt to put food on the table, but hunting today is a recreational pastime, and worse: waterfowl, pheasant, and dove hunting are no more than shooting at living targets. Some hunting is done solely to acquire trophies or to see who can kill the most; some is no more than shooting tame, confined animals. Brutally inhumane weapons such as the bow and arrow are increasingly used. In all cases, sport hunting inflicts undeniable cruelty—pain, trauma, wounding, and death—on living, sentient creatures. Most civilized and caring people will believe that causing suffering and death is by definition inhumane, regardless of method.

More than 100 million animals are reported killed by hunters each year. That number does not include the millions of animals for which kill figures are not maintained by state wildlife agencies. The vast majority of species that are hunted—waterfowl, upland birds, mourning doves, squirrels, raccoons, rabbits, crows, coyotes, etc.—provide minimal sustenance and do not require population control.

Hunters have strived for decades to convince the American public that hunting is good for wildlife and good for society, often with arguments that are based on obfuscation and half-truths. They have deliberately focused the debate on deer hunting, for which plausible, but not necessarily true, argu-

Delaware Action for Animals, "Animals Killed for Sport/Fashion: Hunting," 2005. Reproduced by permission. www.da4a.org/hunting.htm.

ments for subsistence and management can be made. But the holes in their arguments are becoming increasingly apparent, as is the magnitude of their waste, cruelty and destruction. More than that, sport hunting—the killing of wild animals as recreation—is fundamentally at odds with the values of a humane, just and caring society.

Canned Hunting

Canned hunting is the killing of an animal in an enclosure to obtain a trophy. The animals are sometimes tame exotic mammals; some, in fact, have been sold by petting zoos to the canned hunting operation. These animals do not know to run from humans. Many groups that support hunting scorn canned hunting for its unsportsmanlike practice; patrons are guaranteed a kill. Several states now ban canned hunting operations, but the practice is spreading.

From Maine to Arkansas and Indiana to Texas, canned hunting operations are sprouting up all over. The Humane Society of the United States estimates there are more than 1,000 canned hunt operations in at least 25 different states. They are most common in Texas, but they are found throughout the continental United States and Hawaii. Safari Club International (SCI) has done its part to promote canned hunting by creating a hunting achievement award, "Introduced Trophy Game Animals of North America," which may support the operation of canned hunts.

The sale of exotic mammals to canned hunts is big business for private breeders, animal dealers, and disreputable zoos. The over-breeding of captive exotic animals exacerbates the problem. The indiscriminate breeding produces surplus animals, which are then sold, traded, or otherwise disposed of to exhibitors, circuses, animal dealers, game ranches, or individuals. Hunt operators can purchase animals directly through dealers or at auctions. Until those who own exotic animals stop their irresponsible breeding, there will be a steady supply of victims for canned hunting operators.

The killing of a confined or restrained wild animal is abuse for the sake of amusement.

Clients pay large sums of money to participate in canned hunts, which take place in a confined area from which the animal cannot escape. The victims are exotic (non-indigenous) animals, including several varieties of goats and sheep; numerous species of Asian and African antelope; deer, cattle, and swine; and bears, zebra, and sometimes even big cats.

The killing of a confined or restrained wild animal is abuse for the sake of amusement. Unlike situations in which animals can use their natural and instinctual abilities to escape predation, a canned hunt affords animals no such opportunity. In fact, animals may be hand-reared, fed at regular times, and moved regularly among a system of corrals and paddocks. These practices lessen the natural fear and flight response elicited by human beings, and ensure the hunters an easy target. Animals may be set up for a kill as they gather at a regular feeding area or as they move toward a familiar vehicle or person. Once a pattern is established, even the most wary antelope can be manipulated effectively, guaranteeing a kill.

Most states allow canned hunting. Only California, Indiana, Maryland, Nevada, New Jersey, North Carolina, Oregon, Rhode Island, Wisconsin, and Wyoming have laws prohibiting the hunting of exotic mammals in enclosures. Oregon's Fish and Wildlife Commission, responding to public disgust for canned hunting, recently passed a ban on the practice.

At this time, no federal law governs canned hunting. The Animal Welfare Act does not regulate game preserves, hunting preserves, or canned hunts. Although the Endangered Species Act protects species of animals listed as endangered or threatened, it does not prohibit private ownership of endangered animals and may even allow the hunting of endangered species. Federal legislation regarding canned hunts is anticipated in the near future.

Trophy Hunting

Every year, tens of thousands of wild animals, representing hundreds of different species, are killed by American trophy hunters in foreign countries. The heads, hides, tusks, and other body parts of most of these animals are legally imported to the United States by the hunters.

Many animals imported as trophies are members of species protected under the Endangered Species Act (ESA), such as leopards and African elephants. The ESA allows importation of endangered and threatened species only for scientific research, enhancement of propagation, or survival of the species. However, the U.S. Fish and Wildlife Service (FWS), which implements the ESA, has broadly interpreted the term "enhancement" to include trophy hunting of threatened species. While the FWS has rarely allowed the importation of endangered species as trophies, this has not stopped hunters' trophies from making their way across the U.S. border in the guise of scientific research.

Trophy hunting is an elitist hobby, requiring tens of thousands of dollars to participate in each hunting trip.

In 1997, just months after the Smithsonian Institution's National Museum of Natural History accepted a $20 million donation from big-game hunter Kenneth Behring, the Institution sought a FWS permit to import the trophy remains of two endangered wild sheep that Behring shot in Central Asia. One of the sheep, a Kara-Tau argali, is extremely rare in the wild where only 100 exist today. After a storm of ugly publicity, the Smithsonian abandoned the permit application. This was not, however, an isolated case. The Smithsonian has been involved in facilitating the import of endangered species killed by trophy hunters in the past. Other museums have done the same.

While the trophy hunting of endangered and threatened species attracts a great deal of attention, the vast majority of wild animals that American hunters kill and import—such as impala, black bears, common zebra, warthogs, eland, African buffalo, African lions, giraffes, and baboons—are not protected under the ESA or any other domestic law. If the foreign government allows the animals to be killed, as many do, the American hunter can import the trophies.

Trophy hunting is an elitist hobby, requiring tens of thousands of dollars to participate in each hunting trip. Many trophy hunters belong to organizations which promote and enable the so-called "sport," such as Safari Club International (SCI). Founded in 1971, SCI is based in Tucson, Arizona, and has more than 100 chapters in foreign countries. It has a wealthy membership, many of whom are doctors, lawyers and executives, 55% of whom have an annual income exceeding $100,000. SCI's annual conventions attract thousands of current and would-be trophy hunters. Through its publications and conventions, SCI entices people into booking more hunts and helps to hook up the hunting clients with the industry representatives, including outfitters, professional hunters, gun manufacturers and taxidermists. SCI's thick, glossy, bimonthly magazine, *Safari,* contains page after page of advertisements for trophy hunts and [Ernest] Hemingway-like stories glorifying the hunt.

SCI also conducts elite competitions that provide trophy hunters with a playing field so that they can compete with others to kill the most animals of a particular type—one victim from all the bear species in the world, for example. There are 29 awards in all, and in order to win all of them, at the highest level, a hunter would have to kill 322 animals of different species or subspecies. Not the only club of its type, SCI is by far the most prominent trophy-hunting advocacy organization in the world. It protects the hunter in every conceivable forum, including lobbying the U.S. Congress to weaken laws, like the ESA, and lobbying the FWS not to list species that hunters like to kill, such as argali sheep, under the ESA.

Zoos Are Unnecessary and Should Be Discontinued

Richard Fagerlund

Richard Fagerlund is a former columnist for the New Mexico Daily Lobo, *a newspaper published by the University of New Mexico, in Albuquerque.*

I took off work [recently] and visited the zoo with a friend of mine. . . . It was the first time I have been there in 15 years, and it is still as depressing now as it was then. Somehow I think zoos have lost their relevancy in our society. Years ago, we went to zoos to see different exotic animals, but now you can see almost any animal in the world on the internet or on cable or satellite television.

Zoos Unnecessary

It is no longer necessary to keep elephants, giraffes, lions, tigers, zebras and all sorts of other exotic animals in very small enclosures as everyone knows what they look like. When we visited the zoo, we noticed that most of the animals were well fed, and a few had suitable cages or living areas; however, many animals are in substandard housing, based on what they need.

The Bengal tiger paces impatiently around a small cage while being gawked at all day. The Indian elephant, which was rescued from an inhumane circus, simply stands in one place swaying back and forth, a sign of a mental breakdown and impending insanity. This poor creature shouldn't be exposed to the public. She should be cared for in private, so she can get over her ordeal. Elephants are social animals and shouldn't be confined in zoos only to be stared at all day, nor should they be forced to perform stupid circus tricks.

Richard Fagerlund, "Zoos Foster Animal Cruelty," *New Mexico Daily Lobo*, July 3, 2003. Reproduced by permission. http://media.www.dailylobo.com/media/storage/paper344/news/2003/07/03/Opinion/Column.Zoos.Foster.Animal.Cruelty-446117.shtml.

Why do we need to see birds in cages where they have no room to fly? Why are common reptiles and amphibians being held in captivity? Who is going to go home from a trip to the zoo and say they got to see a rufous beaked snake? Most of the reptiles, amphibians and birds would be better off left alone where they normally live. Komodo dragons, Galapagos tortoises and a few others have restricted habitats, but most of the species we saw are not rare and have no business being in captivity.

There probably isn't a person on the planet that doesn't know what an elephant, a rhinoceros, a lion or a tiger looks like.

Zoos are always strapped for money and in some cases they sell their animals for extra income. Some of the animals are sold to ranchers who then sell hunting permits so people can go out and shoot exotic animals without leaving the country. I don't know of any instance where that has happened at the Rio Grande Zoo, but it certainly has happened in other zoos around the country. If zoos would restrict the animals they keep to animals that need help, then they would have more than enough money to run their establishments.

Instead of having a zoo in every major city, we should have a few good zoos around the country that have the animals' best interests in mind, not the viewing public. There probably isn't a person on the planet that doesn't know what an elephant, a rhinoceros, a lion or a tiger looks like. Many wonderful shows on TV offer the opportunity to view all of these animals and others in their natural habitat. We don't need to go to a zoo to see a borderline insane elephant swaying side to side or polar bears trying to keep cool in the summer sun when they would be better off in the arctic. What is the pleasure of watching a tiger pace incessantly around a small cage or a herd of giraffes living in a small enclosure?

Zoos No Longer Relevant

Zoos had importance many years ago but are no longer relevant in our lives. They should start spaying and neutering their animals so we don't keep having baby giraffes born in captivity that will never see the plains of Africa. As the common zoo animals die off, let them go and concentrate on endangered or threatened animals. That will make zoos relevant again. . . .

All in all, the entire zoo trip was very depressing, and it will be a long time before I go again.

Rodeos Are Sanctioned Animal Abuse and Should Be Stopped

Angela Timmons

Angela Timmons is a former reporter and blogger for the Daily Toreador, *the student newspaper of Texas Tech University.*

M y dad, from a small town outside of Matador [Texas] . . . , used to ride bulls. So did other members of my extended family. When my parents moved to Amarillo from New York in 2001, I knew Texas would be a bit of a culture shock. It wasn't all that bad, as I was already accustomed to my father's West Texas ways: the slow drawl and random farm animal noises he regularly enlisted to entertain my northern friends. Cowboy hats and drawls I could handle. There was, however, one thing I refused to embrace, no matter how many times my parents begged me to: the rodeo.

A *Washington Post* article on April 7 [2004] touted bull riding, only one of several rodeo sports, as "America's original extreme sport." In this day and age of dangerous and extreme sports, Americans are apparently saddling up to their televisions to watch "men" engage in the most dangerous eight seconds of their lives. The *Post* reported Nielsen ratings [ratings showing the numbers of television viewers] that show bull riding now brings in more viewers than NBA [National Basketball Association] games.

This hit close to home when the ABC Rodeo bucked into the Lubbock [Texas] Coliseum [recently]. The mere presence of the rodeo was painful for me. But it is the pain the animals endure that concerns me beyond what I can explain in this column. Driving to work one rainy, windy day, I passed horses tied up to trucks, just standing there in the rain, dangerously close to Brownfield Highway traffic. I knew then I had to learn more about rodeo abuses. "Aw, it doesn't hurt 'em," is a statement several of my relatives in the area have used to convince me that rodeo sports are not harmful to animals. I'm not convinced.

Videos of Abuse

Showing Animals Respect and Kindness (SHARK), an organization that investigates animal cruelty, found alarming and heart breaking videos of rodeo abuses throughout the nation. SHARK provides videos and a long list of documented occasions when the horror of rodeo abuse was found.

What are a few of these horrors?

I remember seeing calf roping on television when I was very young; I have refused to view it willingly since, and the image still haunts me. The words to describe how ridiculous this particular sport is escape me. Roping calves are typically three to four months old—mere babies. These babies are repeatedly subjected to acts of cruelty: they are violently roped, normally becoming airborne, and slammed into the ground. Then, the rodeo contestant picks the baby up and slams it on the ground again, and ties up its tiny legs. All the while, its neck is squeezed by the rope tightly circling it.

Any man . . . who uses calf roping to prove masculinity is no man at all.

As SHARK states, if this were done to cats or dogs the same young age as these calves, the offender would probably face charges. But calf ropers get to perform their atrocities on television and in front of screaming fans. Last I checked, the Lubbock Coliseum and other rodeo arenas aren't "out on the ranch" where runaway calves are roped to stay with the crew and not for cruel amusement. Any man (or woman, as the case may be) who uses calf roping to prove masculinity is no man at all. They're not even human.

Tail Twisting, Pulling, and Raking

This was an aspect of rodeo sports I had to look into because I had never heard of it. This involves the raking, pulling or twisting of one of an animal's most sensitive body parts: its tail. The pulling, twisting and raking are done to make calves and steers run chaotically from their enclosed chutes. SHARK caught rodeo contestants, even in the Olympic rodeo of 2002, using these methods to agitate the animals and make them more hostile.

Now, let me ask you something, cowboys: if someone yanked the most sensitive part of your body . . . over a fence, would you become hostile too? Probably. But not to worry—you would soon forget about your anguish when someone came along to slam you down on the ground while you were still in pain, tie up your hands and feet, and throw you around a few more times. Then you would be defenseless and in so much pain, you might just stop breathing. You would probably suffer a few broken bones and torn muscles, and maybe even die. All in the name of sport.

Beating Animals

While probably fairly uncommon in televised rodeos, a SHARK investigator documented a rodeo horse named Cinnebar being beaten to make the animal buck when it initially refused to. Cinnebar was kicked and punched, slapped and had his ears pulled. He was even kicked in the face.

Another discovery for me was the use of electric prods in rodeos, which send about 5,000 volts of painful shocks into the animals. These prods are used to make the animals buck and run, contorting their bodies into the unnatural forms we often see flailing through rodeo arenas. Shocking just made rodeo cruelty all the more shocking to me. . . . I do not have room to discuss all the exploits of rodeo cruelty. At SHARK's Web site, anybody can view numerous videos documenting cruelty the investigators have captured. But people should not need videos to convince them of the cruelty involved in this "sport." This is not a sport—this is sanctioned abuse. Animals are defenseless—even the largest, most powerful animals are defenseless to the cruel mechanisms designed by humans. Humans are the real danger here. That anyone would consciously harm an innocent, living creature is unthinkable. How did such unspeakable abuse ever become OK?

If Americans want to watch "extreme" sports, let's cut out the rodeo and let humans beat . . . each other. At least then they'd be picking on someone their own size.

Organizations to Contact

The editors have compiled the following list of organizations concerned with the issues debated in this book. The descriptions are derived from materials provided by the organizations. All have publications or information available for interested readers. The list was compiled on the date of publication of the present volume; the information provided here may change. Readers need to remember that many organizations take several weeks or longer to respond to inquiries.

The American Anti-Vivisection Society (AAVS)
Noble Plaza, Suite 204, 801 Old York Rd.
Jenkintown, PA   19046-1685
(215) 887-0816
Web site: www.aavs.org

AAVS advocates the abolition of vivisection, a term used to describe the experimental cutting of an animal. It also opposes all types of experiments on living animals and sponsors research on alternatives to these methods. The society's Web site contains useful background essays on various topics, including animal research, animals in education, and the laws governing animal research. The group also publishes the bimonthly *AV Magazine*.

The American Society for the Prevention of Cruelty to Animals (ASPCA)
424 E. Ninety-second St., New York, NY   10128
(212) 876-7700
Web site: www.aspca.org

The ASPCA promotes appreciation for and humane treatment of animals, encourages enforcement of anticruelty laws, and works for the passage of legislation that strengthens existing laws to further protect animals. The ASPCA Web site provides news about animal abuse, information and expert advice about how to take care of many different animals, as well as suggestions on ways to stop animal cruelty.

Americans for Medical Progress

908 King St., Suite 301, Alexandria, VA   22314
(703) 836-9595 • fax: (703) 836-9594
e-mail: info@amprogress.org
Web site: www.amprogress.org

Americans for Medical Progress is a nonprofit organization that works to educate the public about medical research using animals and its importance to curing today's most devastating diseases. Its Web site highlights current media articles regarding the use of animals in research as well as links to other Web sites and fact sheets, such as *Animal Research Facts: Debunking the Myths* and *Rights Versus Welfare: Animal Rights Is Not Animal Welfare.*

Animal Liberation Front (ALF)

6320 Canoga Ave., Woodland Hills, CA   91367
(818) 227-5022
e-mail: press@animalliberationpressoffice.org
Web site: http://animalliberationfront.com/

The Animal Liberation Front carries out direct action against animal abuse by rescuing animals from farms and medical facilities and by causing financial loss to companies and individuals it considers to be animal exploiters, usually through the damage and destruction of property. ALF seeks to save as many animals as possible and disrupt the practice of animal abuse, but its long-term aim is to end all animal suffering by forcing abusing companies out of business. Its Web site contains links to numerous publications on animal rights, information about the animal rights philosophy, and suggestions for animal activism.

Farm Sanctuary

PO Box 150, Watkins Glen, NY 14891

fax: (607) 583-2041

Web site: www.farmsanctuary.org

Farm Sanctuary is a nonprofit organization dedicated to ending the use of animals for food production. It works through grassroots campaigns and operates rescue and rehabilitation shelters for farm animals. Its Web site offers information and photos about such issues as factory farming, proposed legislation, and litigation relating to animal cruelty on farms. The organization publishes the quarterly *Sanctuary News.*

Foundation for Biomedical Research (FBR)

818 Connecticut Ave. NW, Suite 900, Washington, DC 20006

(202) 457-0654 • fax: (202) 457-0659

Web site: www.fbresearch.org

FBR provides information and educational programs about what it sees as the necessary and important role of laboratory animals in biomedical research and testing. Its brochures include *Proud Achievements of Animal Research* and *Fact vs. Myth About the Essential Need for Animals in Medical Research.*

Fur Commission USA

826 Orange Ave., #506, Coronado, CA 92118

(619) 575-0319 • fax: (619) 575-5578

e-mail: furfarmers@aol.com

Web site: www.furcommission.org

Fur Commission USA is a nonprofit national association representing U.S. mink and fox farmers. Its goal is to educate the public about responsible fur farming. The commission's Web site provides information about various aspects of the U.S. fur industry, including such topics as humane euthanasia. It also offers several educational tools for all ages on fur farming, including the educational kit *Animals and Our Clothing.*

The Humane Society of the United States (HSUS)
2100 L St. NW, Washington, DC   20037
(202) 452-1100
Web site: www.hsus.org

HSUS works to foster respect, understanding, and compassion for all creatures. It maintains programs that support responsible pet ownership, eliminating cruelty in hunting and trapping, and exposing abuses of animals in research and testing and in movies, circuses, pulling contests, and racing. It campaigns for and against legislation affecting animal protection and monitors enforcement of existing animal-protection statutes. HSUS publishes the quarterly *All Animals,* the *Pain and Distress Report,* and the *Animal Research News & Analysis Newsletter.*

National Association for Biomedical Research (NABR)
818 Connecticut Ave. NW, Suite 900, Washington, DC   20006
(202) 857-0540 • fax: (202) 659-1902
Web site: www.nabr.org

NABR supports the responsible use and humane care and treatment of laboratory animals in research, education, and product safety testing. Further, the membership believes that only as many animals as necessary should be used; that any pain or distress animals may experience should be minimized; and that alternatives to the use of live animals should be developed and employed wherever feasible.

People for the Ethical Treatment of Animals (PETA)
501 Front St., Norfolk, VA   23510
(757) 622-7382 • fax: (757) 622-0457
e-mail: peta@norfolk.infi.net
Web site: www.peta-online.org

An international animal rights organization, PETA is dedicated to establishing and protecting the rights of all animals. It focuses on four areas: factory farms, research laboratories, the fur trade, and the entertainment industry. PETA promotes public education, cruelty investigations, animal rescue, celebrity involvement, and legislative and direct action. Its Web site offers numerous videos showing animals at factory farms and slaughterhouses as well as various fact sheets, brochures, and essays about animal rights.

Performing Animal Welfare Society (PAWS)

PO Box 849, Galt, CA 95632
(209) 745-2606 • fax: (209) 745-1809
e-mail: info@paws.org
Web site: www.paws.org/

Founded in 1985, PAWS provides sanctuary to abandoned and abused performing animals and victims of the exotic pet trade. The society also works to protect animals by educating the public about inhumane animal training and treatment. Its Web site contains numerous fact sheets about protecting and caring for domesticated as well as wild animals, and the group publishes several newsletters, such as *Wild Again* and the monthly *PAWS Magazine*.

Physicians Committee for Responsible Medicine (PCRM)

5100 Wisconsin Ave., Suite 400, Washington, DC 20016
(202) 686-2210
e-mail: pcrm@pcrm.org
Web site: www.pcrm.org

PCRM is a nonprofit organization supported by both physicians and laypersons to encourage higher ethical standards and effectiveness in research. It promotes using computer programs and models in place of animals in both research and education. The committee publishes the quarterly magazine *Good Medicine* and numerous fact sheets on animal experimentation issues.

Society & Animals Forum

PO Box 1257, Washington Grove, MD 20880
(301) 963-4751 • fax: (301) 963-4751

e-mail: kshapiro@societyandanimalsforum.org
Web site: www.psyeta.org

The Society & Animals Forum, formerly called Psychologists for the Ethical Treatment of Animals, seeks to ensure proper treatment for animals used in psychological research and education. Thus, it urges schools to include information about ethical issues in the treatment of animals in their curricula, works to reduce the number of animals needed for experiments, and has developed a tool to measure the level of invasiveness or severity of animal experiments. Its Web site contains reviews of relevant books and summaries of articles from the journals *Society and Animals* and *Journal of Applied Animal Welfare Science.* The group also publishes *Society and Animals Forum Newsletter.*

Bibliography

Books

The Animal Studies Group	*Killing Animals.* Champaign: University of Illinois Press, 2006.
Arnold Arluke	*Brute Force: Policing Animal Cruelty.* West Lafeyette, IN: Purdue University Press, 2007.
Diane L. Beers	*For the Prevention of Cruelty: The History and Legacy of Animal Rights Activism in the United States.* Athens, OH: Swallow Press, 2006.
Marc Bekoff and Jane Goodall	*Animals Matter: A Biologist Explains Why We Should Treat Animals with Compassion and Respect.* Boston: Shambhala, 2007.
Carl Cohen	*The Animal Rights Debate.* Lanham, MD: Rowman & Littlefield, 2001.
Gary Francione	*Introduction to Animal Rights: Your Child or Your Dog?* Philadelphia: Temple University Press, 2000.
Julian H. Franklin	*Animal Rights and Moral Philosophy.* New York: Columbia University Press, 2006.
Catherine Grant	*The No-nonsense Guide to Animal Rights.* Oxford, UK: New Internationalist, 2006.

| Allison Hills | *Do Animals Have Rights?* Cambridge, UK: Totem Press, 2006. |

| Linda Kalof and Amy Fitzgerald | *The Animals Reader: The Essential Classic and Contemporary Writings.* Oxford, UK: Berg, 2007. |

| Tom Regan | *The Case for Animal Rights.* Berkeley and Los Angeles: University of California Press, 2004. |

| Tom Regan | *Defending Animal Rights.* Champaign: University of Illinois Press, 2006. |

| Bernard E. Rollin | *Animal Rights and Human Morality.* Amherst, NY: Prometheus Books, 2006. |

| Bernard E. Rollin | *Farm Animal Welfare: Social, Bioethical, and Research Issues.* Hoboken, NJ: Wiley-Blackwell, 2003. |

| Roger Scruton | *Animal Rights and Wrongs.* New York: Continuum International, 2006. |

| Peter Singer | *Animal Liberation.* New York: HarperPerennial, 2001. |

| Peter Singer | *In Defense of Animals: The Second Wave.* Hoboken, NJ: Wiley-Blackwell, 2005. |

| Peter Singer | *The Way We Eat: Why Our Food Choices Matter.* Emmaus, PA: Rodale Press, 2006. |

| Cass R. Sunstein and Martha Nussbaum | *Animal Rights: Current Debates and New Directions.* New York: Oxford University Press, 2005. |

| Erin E. Williams and Margo Demello | *Why Animals Matter: The Case for Animal Protection.* Amherst, NY: Prometheus Books, 2007. |

Periodicals

Jerry Adler and Tara Weingarten	"A Flap over Foie Gras: Chefs—and Diners—Love the Fatty Duck Liver, but Animal-Rights Activists Are Crying Fowl at the Birds' Treatment," *Newsweek*, May 2, 2005.
Mark Bittman	"Rethinking the Meat-Guzzler," *New York Times*, January 27, 2008. www.nytimes.com/2008/01/27/weekin review/27bittman.html?-r=1&oref= slogin.
Economist	"Good News for Humans; Animal Rights," July 29, 2006.
Alex Epstein	"The Terror of 'Animal Rights,'" *Bucks County (PA)Courier Times*, February 16, 2004.
Fulton County (GA) Daily Report	"Animal Rights Litigation Grows Throughout U.S.," June 6, 2007.
Chris Kirkham	"Fish Factories," *New Orleans Times-Picayune*, December 9, 2007 http://tinyurl.com/32sqqo.
Andrey Kobilnyk	"Do Animals Have Rights?" *First Science.com*, October 1, 2007. www.firstscience.com/home/perspec tives/editorials/do-animals-have-ri ghts_37122.html.

Eva Kooyman   "How Does It End Up on My Plate?"
                            Earth Focus: One Planet-One Com-
                            munity, Summer 2005.

Michael D.   "Who Belongs in the Zoo?" *Time,*
Lemonick   June 19, 2006.

Eugene Linden   "How Much Do Animals Really
                            Know?" *Parade* July 29, 2007.
                            www.parade.com/articles/editions/
                            2007/edition_07-29-2007/Anim
                            al_Intelligence.

Trent Loos   "Kids or Pigs: You Decide," *Feedstuffs,*
                            November 6, 2006.

Megan McArdle   "Animal Rights," *The Atlantic.com,*
                            August 22, 2007. http://
                            meganmcardle.theatlantic.com/
                            archives/2007/08/as_long_time_read
                            ers_know.php.

John J. Miller   "In the Name of the Animals:
                            America Faces a New Kind of Terror-
                            ism," *National Review,* July 3, 2006.

Newsweek   "What We Owe What We Eat: Why,
                            Matthew Scully Asks, Is Cruelty to a
                            Puppy Appalling and Cruelty to Live-
                            stock by the Billions a Matter of So-
                            cial Indifference?" July 18, 2005.

Christian Nolan   "Pets More than Just Property?" *Con-*
                            necticut Law Tribune, June 11, 2007.

Bailey Norwood,
Jayson Lusk, and
Robert Prickett

"Consumers Share Views on Farm Animal Welfare: Survey Looks into What Consumers Think About Various Farm Animal Welfare Issues," *Feedstuffs*, October 8, 2007.

Keith Nunes

"F.D.A. Declares Food from Cloned Animals Is Safe," *Meat & Poultry*, January 15, 2008. http://www.meat poultry.com/news/daily_enews.asp? ArticleID=90649.

Ed Owen

"The Dangers of Cuddly Extremism: By Their Emotive Rejection of All Animal Testing, the Mainstream Animal Rights Organisations Are Providing Encouragement for the Violent Fringe," *New Statesman*, September 12, 2005.

People Weekly

"Horse Rescuer: Neda DeMayo Battles the Government to Stop the Roundup—and Slaughter—of Wild Horses," May 9, 2005.

Michael Pollan

"An Animal's Place," *New York Times*, November 10, 2002. http://query.ny times.com/gst/fullpage.html?res= 9500EFD7153EF933A25752C1 A9649C 8B63.

Margot Roosevelt

"Campaign '06: Treating Pigs Better in Arizona," *Time*, November 6, 2007.

Wesley J. Smith   "Animal Planet: Animal-Rights Terrorism Is on the Increase and Animal-Rights Activists Aren't Doing Enough to Stop It," *Weekly Standard*, May 24, 2006.

Index

A

Abolitionist viewpoint of animals, 31, 36–37, 117

Abuse of animals
through anthropomorphism, 75
bullfighting, 174
canned hunting, 178
at free-range farms, 113
by humans, 29, 68, 71
through research, 126, 145
in rodeos, 185–188
shelter dogs/cats, 73
slaughterhouses, 120
vs. veganism, 118
See also Animal welfare, mistreatment; Violence

Acquired immune deficiency syndrome (AIDS), 131, 140, 148

Activism for animal rights
against agriculture industry, 16
economic role of, 109
vs. exploitation, 96
against factory farms, 112
medical research/testing, 150–151
radical activities, 113–114
reigning in, 109–110
by students, 112–113
targets of, 16–17
values of, 66
violence by, 17–18, 66, 68, 71

Advocacy views
on animal experimentation, 24
on animal welfare, 17, 23–24, 27–28

against humans, 133
on violence, 17–18

AgriProcessors (video), 82

Allen, Arthur, 150–154

Alzheimer's disease, 154

American Veterinary Medical Association (AVMA), 22, 90, 94–95, 109

Anderegg, Christopher, 137–146

Andreas, Daniel, 18

Animal agriculture
animal-borne diseases in, 100
captive-bolt euthanasia, 95–96
consumer understanding, 101–102
dissolution of, 31–32, 37, 90–91
farmer/rancher protection, 96–97
food security and, 104
HSUS and, 102
legislation against, 102–103
livestock, 80, 92–96, 102, 135, 168
for low-cost food, 101–104
vs. pet ownership, 102–103
welfare concerns, 92–97
See also Chicken farming; Factory farms; Farming

Animal Defenders International, 167

Animal Enterprise Terrorism Act, 17

Animal experimentation and research
advocacy on, 24
benefits of, 126
on bioethics, 124

into resistant diseases, 99
side effects of, 143, 153
of stem cells, animal, 136
into toxicity, 152–153
into vaccines, 134
See also Animal experimentation and research; Medical research/testing

E

Ecological balance, 111, 172–174
Economic role of animals
activism role in, 109
in agricultural industry, 92
in bullfighting, 172–174
cage-free trends, 107
experimentation for, 144, 146
importance of, 21–23
international impact of, 29
in marine ecology, 111
Einstein, Albert, 118
Elan Pharmaceuticals, 154
Electric prods, 187–188
Elephant's emotions, 53
Emotions
in animals, 49–50, 53–54, 76, 119
human to animal, 42, 75
in humans, 51, 95–96
vs. industry regulations, 96
interpretation of, 45
vs. reason, 33, 36
suffering as, 146
Empathy problems, 44–45, 51
Endangered Species Act (ESA), 179–181
Entertainment
bear hunting as, 162–164
bullfighting as, 171–175
circuses as, 167
growth of, 16–17
horse racing as, 156–158

income from, 28
injuries in, 156–157
performance drugs for, 156
PETA and, 67, 129, 156–157
rescue organizations against, 157
rodeos as, 168–170, 185–188
sport hunting as, 176–181
sportfishing as, 30, 159–161, 160
torture in, 41
training/transport issues, 165
zoos as, 182–184
See also Animal welfare, mistreatment
Epidemiology, nonanimal experimentation, 142
Epstein, Alex, 127–130
Equality, animals *vs.* humans, 40, 65–66, 69, 77, 87
Esselstyn, Caldwell, 142
Ethical dilemma, animal rights debate, 21, 150–154
Euthanasia, 76, 80, 95–96, 157, 168
Exploitation of animals
vs. activists, 96
vs. animal rights, 33–34, 36–38, 75–77
in bullfighting, 171–175
criminal action against, 71
disciplined passion needed for, 38
vs. human rights, 26, 36, 75, 121
implications of, 36–38
moral theory against, 33–34, 69
rights against, 16–17
in rodeos, 185–188
in sport hunting, 176–181
system irregularities of, 31–33